D1570374

MID-YORK *Library System*
1600 Lincoln Avenue Utica, New York 13502

I'm
Not Done
Yet!

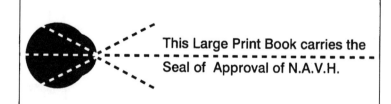

This Large Print Book carries the
Seal of Approval of N.A.V.H.

I'm Not Done Yet!

Keeping at It, Remaining Relevant, and Having the Time of My Life

EDWARD I. KOCH

with Daniel Paisner

Thorndike Press • Thorndike, Maine

Copyright © 2000 by Edward I. Koch

All rights reserved.

Published in 2000 by arrangement with William Morrow, an imprint of HarperCollins Publishers, Inc.

Thorndike Press Large Print Senior Lifestyles Series.

The tree indicium is a trademark of Thorndike Press.

The text of this Large Print edition is unabridged.
Other aspects of the book may vary from the original edition.

Set in 16 pt. Plantin by Anne Bradeen.

Printed in the United States on permanent paper.

Library of Congress Cataloging-in-Publication Data

Koch, Ed, 1924–
    I'm not done yet! : keeping at it, remaining relevant, and having the time of my life / Edward I Koch with Daniel Paisner.
    p. cm.
    Originally published: New York : William Morrow, 2000.
    ISBN 0-7862-2891-1 (lg. print : hc : alk. paper)
    1. Koch, Ed, 1924– 2. Mayors — New York (State) —
New York — Biography. 3. New York (N.Y.) — Politics and government — 1951– 4. New York (N.Y.) — Biography.
I. Paisner, Daniel. II. Title.
F128.54.K63 A3 2000b
974.7'1043'092—dc21
    [B]   00-059973

This book is dedicated to U.S. District Court Judge Allen G. Schwartz, my first law partner (in 1964) and my good friend ever since. Allen served brilliantly in my administration as corporation counsel, the city's lawyer, and I think he was the best the city ever had. I know that he is the best friend I ever had. His intellect is awesome and his courage inspiring.

Acknowledgments

My collaborator on this book, Dan Paisner, is someone I have known since 1991, when we wrote my autobiography, *Citizen Koch*. I take great pride in my writing skills, and I had no hesitation in joining with Dan because what he brings to the assignment is a brilliant editor's intellect and great ability to organize. He knows the areas that have to be covered, and he is able to focus my mind. He recorded our many conversations and prompted me with questions, so we could be sure my recollections did not become simply a stream of consciousness. He certainly did his job, as I hope you will agree when you hear my voice on every page.

When the manuscript was put in draft form and circulated among my close friends for their input, they liked it and made suggestions (some of which I took; others, I didn't). Their observations were all very important in arriving at the final product. Those friends are Allen G. Schwartz, James F. Gill, Henry J. Stern, Clark Whelton,

Austin Campriello, and my sister, Pat Thaler. I am truly appreciative of their involvement.

Thanks are also due to Dan Strone of the William Morris Agency, for helping to get this book off the ground, and to Michael Gershenson, First Vice President — Investments at PaineWebber, for his contributions on financial matters relating to retirement planning.

I think the reaction of my editor, Paul Bresnick — who, after reading the book, called me to say "I like it!" and required nothing further from me — was the result, first, of Dan Paisner's expertise and insights and, second, of the comments of the friends who had taken the time to read the draft and provide suggestions. I find writing to be lots of fun, and I hope you will enjoy reading what we have written as much as we enjoyed writing it.

Contents

One

Remaining Relevant

As I write this, I've been out of office now for close to ten years, and on my next birthday I'll be seventy-five years old. Seventy-five! And yet I can't recall a time in my life when I've felt stronger, looked better, worked harder, or enjoyed myself any more than right now. I've always thought it was a bit ridiculous (and not to be believed) when people tell you they're having the time of their life, but I've got to admit these past few years have been very special — and some of my best years to date.

I realize, of course, that nothing I ever do will approach the elation I experienced for twelve years as mayor of the greatest, most vibrant, and (potentially) most volatile city on the planet. And I realize, too, that I will never again sleep through the night without having to get up to urinate four times in the hours just before dawn — at least not on anything like a regular basis. (In this one respect, at least, I am living testimony to what President Bill Clinton told Monica Lewinsky would ultimately happen to him . . . the prostate does all us males in!) Naturally, these two realizations are not interconnected, except insofar as they impact on me. But that's precisely the point — they do impact on me, and in a big way, too.

I'm not deluding myself. Things have changed, I have changed, the world has changed around me. What I once took for granted I now spend time thinking about. The best, most fulfilling years of my professional life are certainly behind me, just as the best, most full-functioning years of my physical life are behind me as well. But I'm here to report that there are indeed other hills to climb after reaching your professional and physical peaks. There are thrills to be had, goals to be met, causes to be championed, and footprints to be left behind. My personal "bests" are behind me, but there are many more "very goods" to come.

Of course, my career peak was being elected mayor of the City of New York in

1977, after a long career as a New York City congressman, councilman, Democratic party district leader in Greenwich Village, and attorney in private practice. Serving out my three mayoral terms during one of the most exciting times in the city's history topped it all. I'll leave it to history to judge whether I served those three terms with distinction, but let me tell you, being entrusted with the good and welfare of seven and a half million New Yorkers was an honor and a challenge like no other, and working to meet that challenge was its own special reward. It would be foolish to try to match that period in my life. At the same time, however, it would be ridiculous to throw in the towel after such an extraordinary experience — to step back, shut down, and tune out of the very community I helped to sustain, and in some instances created. Having had tremendous impact at one point does not mean you should look away from having some lesser impact at a later point; or, in more poetic terms, having danced at the top doesn't foreclose continuing the dance of a meaningful life, even if at a somewhat slower pace.

It would also be foolish to attempt to match my physical powers with those I once enjoyed. I have done foolish things in my lifetime (haven't we all?), but I am not a fool and have never misled myself into thinking I can move with the same speed and devil-take-the-hindmost attitude I had as a young man. The cruel truth is my body no longer does what I want it to all the time, and sometimes it's inclined to do its own thing independent of my wishes. My physical peak was at age nineteen, more than thirty years before I was elected mayor, when I was drafted into the army and assigned to seventeen weeks of basic training at Camp Croft in Spartanburg, South Carolina. As I have often noted, I was never much of an athlete, even as a child. My favorite running comment on the matter, which I began using after becoming mayor to explain my lack of interest in baseball, was an apocryphal line I attributed to my mother. According to the story, she was always saying to me and my brother, "Harold, you go outside and play baseball. Eddie, you sit in the corner and study to be mayor."

A word or two on my time in Spartanburg. It was the spring of 1943, and I was a lanky nineteen-year-old from Ocean Parkway in Brooklyn. I didn't play sports, I hardly understood them, and they held little interest beyond the aspects of character they sometimes revealed about some of my cohorts.

My brother Harold was a superb athlete, but I never believed it was because I couldn't compete with him that I shied away from competitive sports. I just wasn't interested. I went down to South Carolina weighing about 185 pounds, and at the end of seventeen weeks I was down to about 160. It was 110 degrees in the shade almost every day, and if it dropped to 90 degrees, as it did on occasion, I had to wear a field jacket because I felt cold. (Today I would settle for 200 pounds. I'm always on a diet; as of this writing, I weigh 222 pounds.) Everything is relative. When I was later sent to Camp Carson in Colorado, joining the 104th Combat Infantry Division, which had just come off maneuvers in southern California, I stood out like the skinny, naïve kid I truly was, thrown in with a group of tanned, tough G.I.s, many of them from the Deep South. But I was as fit as I would ever be and more sure of myself physically than I had ever been. A few weeks before completing basic training, I had engaged in a boxing match with a fellow squad member who made anti-Semitic remarks about some of the Jews in the platoon. He beat me, I feel compelled to note, but the anti-Semitic remarks ended, and I felt terrific that I had taken him on.

The space between 1943 and 1999 is not as huge as it might seem, although in this one respect it might as well be the stretch of time between the Paleozoic era and the Jurassic. Since I weigh 222 pounds, the only obstacle course I'm likely to complete is one that involves a beeline to the men's room. I've weighed as much as 240 pounds (during my last term as mayor). I've had a stroke. I have a pacemaker to correct an erratic heartbeat. I take ten different prescription medications every day: one to keep my blood thin, another for my benign prostate condition, several beta-based drugs for my arrhythmia . . . you get the idea. I've been on more diets than I care to count, and lost more pounds, cumulatively, than the combined inaugural weights of my successors as mayor. I work out at a gym daily (I'll go through my exercise regimen later on in these pages), but one unending struggle for me has been to control my weight. Some people give up, but I never will. Every day is a new day when I say to myself, "Let the battle begin."

All in all, I find it hard to accept that I'm seventy-four, and one of the reasons I find it so hard is that I don't feel as if I'm moving about in a seventy-four-year-old body. Despite my various medical problems (and I'll talk about those too, later on), I'm in pretty good shape. I don't *feel* old. And I like to think I don't *look* old. At least, I don't look old to me. The face staring back at me in the mirror is the same face I saw when I was a congressman, give or take a few wrinkles; even the body looks the same, give or take a few pounds. I must confess to a difference between the earlier and later photos of me in our family picture album, but so what? My God, I went to my fiftieth law school reunion at New York University and my classmates looked positively over-the-hill. I thought to myself: I don't look like *that.* And it's not just my own opinion I'm relying on here. People are constantly telling me how good I look, how young I seem, and I don't think it's to humor me. "You look much better alive," they often say in a surprised voice when they meet me for the first time, after which I find myself thinking, Better than what? What they mean to say, obviously, is that I look better in person than I do on television, and I choose to accept this as a compliment. (What choice do I have, really?)

Have you noticed there's always an unspoken qualifier, when people stop to say something nice about your appearance or demeanor? They'll toss in a *considering.* Or, *for your age,* which I hear more and more, the longer I stick around. You look great, *for your age.* You're in tremendous shape, *considering.* You're amazingly active, alert, intuitive . . . *for your age.* I hate the way we have to qualify even so veiled a compliment as this, although by outlasting, outhustling, outdebating, outwitting, and outexercising my contemporaries I have left myself no alternative but to shoulder such faint praise with aplomb. I used to tell people, when I left office back in 1989 and after I lost forty pounds, that I looked like a Greek god, explaining that before my weight loss I looked like a Jewish god. Then I told them my secret: Never, never give up on how you look. For me, it's not simply a health issue, it's a necessary vanity. Without that self-interest or vanity, I believe, the odds of remaining relevant are stacked against you. It's difficult to matter when you don't matter to yourself. And besides, the world doesn't respect a fat man. True, there are exceptions, but I'm referring to the run-of-the-mill.

When I was voted out of office in 1989, I moved quickly to ensure that I wouldn't stagnate or rest on my laurels. A lot of people — at a similar age, in a similar position — might have decided to wind down and find some nonstressful way to earn a living. Others might have gone on the lecture circuit to rehash old times, or found an avocation taking up a few hours a day, or maybe only a couple of days a week. Such a move, for me, was out of the question. I never even considered *retirement*. The word itself, I'm afraid, is enough to age me. Or put me to sleep. I honestly believe that the concept of retirement is responsible for shortened lives. Anyway, I fear that the moment I stop working, stop reaching, stop mattering, is the moment I'm done. I've spent some time thinking about this. You've got to keep the mind active. You've got to keep the body active. Your muscles atrophy if not used, and I believe the brain is like a muscle in that respect and likewise atrophies. You've got to keep your spirit flying.

Working, thinking, debating, assessing, analyzing, criticizing . . . these are my strengths, and I've been fortunate to be able to make a living by way of them. (I even found a way to make money from "judging," as I'll explain later on.) In a sense, I'm working harder now than I did as mayor. I'm actually engaged in nine jobs, at last count, and that number has been as high as eleven. I count as a job only those enterprises that yield an independent revenue stream. If it doesn't bring in money, it's a hobby, and I've never been much for hobbies. I do what I do, and I want to do more. I haven't finished. My friends tell me I take on more than I can handle, but I've never missed a deadline. I've never missed an appointment or failed to deliver on a commitment. I'm very disciplined, and determined to do a good job, whatever it is.

Underlying everything I do is the challenge in getting it done, getting it done right, and being relevant. Since all of us, with the exception of Mother Teresa, have some vanity, I want above all to be relevant in my comments and actions, as perceived by others. And I want to look reasonably good, as perceived by others. Honestly, looking at some of my law school classmates scared the hell out of me. Some were bent over, others had bellies hanging over their belts. I thought, That's not me! I don't want to let simple chronology — the passage of years — or simple indifference be my undoing.

As far as I'm concerned, there is never any time like the present. It is anathema to me to live in the past, and I resist the impulse to do so at every turn. Understand, there are impulses all around — most of them encouraged by questions lobbed by enterprising reporters wanting me to wax nostalgic about my term as mayor, or frustrated New Yorkers wanting me to run again. I don't go down that road. Sure, I look back fondly (and frequently) on some of the more significant moments from my time as mayor, and it doesn't take a detective to notice that my office is decorated with photographs and mementos from my three terms. But the most important course, to me, has always been the present course, the road to a better future. It's what I might do today, or tomorrow, not what I've done yesterday or a few years back. Which was why, when I saw the figures coming in on the night of my last election — the Democratic primary for mayor, on September 12, 1989 — I felt a tremendous sense of relief. Really, that's the best way to describe it. I was in the last months of my third term, and no New York City mayor had ever served a fourth. I ran hoping to win, but as the polls closed and as it became apparent that David Dinkins would claim the party's nomination, I didn't feel any great sense of loss. There was no remorse, no sadness, no wondering *what if* or *what might have been*. It was time to move forward, on to the next thing, even though at the time I had no idea what that next thing might be.

What's interesting to me now is that the

Sheraton Centre hotel suite where most of my friends and supporters had gathered on the night of the primary was a fairly somber room. "Tentative" is a good way to describe the prevailing emotion. My closest advisers were present, along with my closest friends, and my family. These were the people who knew me better than anyone else — although not, it seems, as well as they thought. At the beginning, as the returns started to come in, I was holding a slight lead, but it became quickly apparent that things were starting to look grim. We all knew that the city's white precincts tended to file before the city's black precincts, and a slight lead in these early numbers would not be enough to see me to victory. David Dinkins, being black, was naturally expected to carry the black vote overwhelmingly. (In the end, he tallied 97 percent of the black vote — an extraordinary number.)

When it became clear I had lost, *I* was the one trying to lift everyone's spirits. Many of these good, caring friends were crying, and all had sad faces. I wasn't crying. I wasn't sad. I know it sounds disingenuous, but I truly wasn't. I actually said to myself, in the words of Martin Luther King, Jr.: "Free at last! Free at last! Thank God Almighty, I'm free at last!"

Is there a contradiction here? I don't think so. I wanted to be the first four-term mayor simply because I have a competitive streak and I love a good challenge — and a good fight. And I thought I was a good mayor. I wouldn't have run in the first place if I didn't think I was the best person for the job, and I wouldn't have kept at it so long had the people of New York thought otherwise. However, I also realized that being mayor was shortening my life. I realized that as a result of the time and sweat and effort and *agità* I'd spent on the city's behalf, I would likely die ahead of schedule. Based on the genes I had gotten from my father, who died at eighty-seven after working his whole life, I was expecting a long run, and I didn't mind losing a few years for the opportunity to serve another four as mayor. It seemed like a fair trade, because I believe in public service and have said a thousand times it is the noblest of professions if it's done honestly and done well.

So, while the room at the Sheraton was filled with conflicting emotions, there was no conflict in me — and no contradiction. I could actually feel a great weight being lifted from my shoulders. It was a palpable sensation. Have you ever had that feeling, at the end of a difficult task, when the hard

23

work and pressure are all behind you and all that's left to do is to breathe a long sigh? Some mornings I hate heading out to the gym for my daily workout, but when I'm through I love the feeling of *having* exercised. That's what it was like for me that night at the Sheraton. I had been prepared and even eager to carry that great weight, but that doesn't mean it didn't feel terrific to have it lifted from me just the same. I loved being mayor, and just then I loved the thought of *having been* mayor. Let somebody else carry the burden of New York City for the next while, I said to myself. Let somebody else worry about the budget, crime, our decaying infrastructure, the fate and fortune of seven and a half million New Yorkers. And let that somebody else be David Dinkins. No, I didn't all of a sudden think he was better qualified. But the people had spoken and he was certainly willing, and most people, myself included, thought he was able.

If I had to make the same decision to run for a fourth term today, against the same odds, I'd make it the same way. As it played out, I accepted the outcome without bitterness, for strictly personal reasons, but I would have relished being mayor for another four years, for mostly political reasons

— and to finish projects that I had started. Yet the people closest to me were slow to grasp this distinction. I can understand that. We all assumed I'd win, and I don't say this with any arrogance or braggadocio. It's just that, in any closely fought election, the assumption on both sides is that your side will win — and this is especially so if you happen to be the incumbent. It is an assumption that comes from your confidence in your ability to do the job, and I never really faced the prospect of what I might do if the nomination went to Dinkins. It was unthinkable, in the sense that it never, ever occurred to me.

It hadn't really occurred to those around me either. My brother Harold (who died in August 1995, at the age of seventy-four) told reporters that when the results came in that night he was worried about me. He said he thought my whole life was wrapped up in being mayor, and that he was afraid I might be overwhelmed by the defeat. But he was wrong. My whole life is wrapped up in whatever I'm doing at the time, and it didn't take the finality of those primary returns to get me to realize it. I knew this about myself as surely as I knew my own name.

Let's face it, I was not the only person qualified to be mayor of New York City, just as being mayor of New York City was not the only job I was qualified to do. I am not a perfectionist, and I am not a genius. I'm a very hard worker, and I'm able to do things that geniuses often can't. I can take the idea of a genius and make it happen. As mayor, I surrounded myself with first-rate people, many of them with far better minds than I could ever hope to have, and it didn't bother me at all because I could get things done that they couldn't possibly get done. Most "geniuses" can't fight their way out of a paper bag. They don't have the organizational skills or the discipline to accomplish far-reaching or many-faceted tasks. In many cases, they have too much of an ego to collaborate, or to share the credit, or to sublimate their own interests for a greater good. Whatever I'd go on to do next, I knew I'd do it well because I'd find the best people with whom to do it. It's a formula that transcends politics and government.

I don't mean to gloss over the fact that there is a certain pain in losing so public a battle as an election — especially for so prominent a position as mayor of New York. To be honest, I took it personally that the people of New York had rejected me. (After all I had done for them!) But that's life, that's politics, and I knew I couldn't dwell on it. I decided, unlike many pundits who believed that the racially motivated murder of a young black man six weeks before the election was the cause of my defeat, that it was longevity that did me in. People simply got tired of me after twelve years. I understood that. I didn't like it, but I understood it. So I made a conscious, deliberate decision to set this defeat aside and move on. It wasn't an agonized, labored decision. The alternatives seemed clear that night at the Sheraton. Either you dwell on your defeat and lapse into a depression, or you pull yourself up out of that moment and race headlong into the next one. I chose the latter course — and it really was a no-brainer, as we nongeniuses like to say.

Regrettably, not every politician has such a clear view. Mario Cuomo, I was told, didn't take it too well when he lost the 1994 gubernatorial election to George Pataki. His friends and advisers were worried about his health; he was reportedly depressed. I called him on the telephone a few days after the election, as a veteran "loser," to see if I could be of any help. I'd always had a mixed relationship with Mario Cuomo, not quite a love/hate relationship, which often results when two politicians have a long history of running against each other. In our case, there was not a lot of love, but there was certainly a long history of having worked together. We also shared a close friend and political adviser, David Garth, who signed on to manage my 1977 campaign for mayor after double-checking with then New York Secretary of State Cuomo on his intention to run for the same office. Garth had earlier pledged his services to Cuomo in a campaign for mayor, but Mario had said he wasn't running. Perhaps he couldn't make up his mind so early in the game. Cuomo, as the world would come to know, was never quick to make a political decision, and I used to joke that this early indecision was perhaps the first time it would cost him an election, because once David Garth cast his lot with me there was no stopping us.

Ultimately, Mario Cuomo's campaign managers ran a truly hateful campaign against me in the Democratic primary for mayor in 1977. After my bachelor status gave rise to whispers regarding my sexual preferences, placards appeared all along Queens Boulevard, proclaiming "Vote for Cuomo, Not the Homo!" I suspected right away that some of his people were behind it, and a later report in *The Village Voice* confirmed my suspicions. Now, Mario might not have authorized it directly, but he had to know about it. At the very least, he looked the other way. I've never forgotten that, and he knows it. Five years later, when I went up against him in the Democratic primary for governor, the campaign was carried out on a somewhat higher plane, but it was no less rancorous. There was even another homosexual smear, from one of his upstate campaign managers.

In the end, I was the mayor and he was the governor, and we were forced to get along for the good of the city, the state, and the party. In truth, Mario Cuomo was actually a pretty good governor. He was not a great governor. Hugh Carey was a great governor, but Mario was a good one and when he ran for his fourth term, I supported him. When I was asked to do a commercial for him, I did it without hesitation. I did it because I was asked by David Garth, Cuomo's campaign adviser, and I did it because I felt an obligation to the Democratic Party. I also did it because at the time I thought he was the best man for the job. No matter what invective we had exchanged over the years, there was no denying Cuomo his accomplishments, so I did what I could to help him win.

After Cuomo lost the election to George Pataki, I felt I should offer some comfort. I'd gone through a similar defeat just a few years earlier, and there weren't a whole lot of people he could call on with such common ground. "Mario," I said when I reached him on the phone, "I hear you're depressed, and I don't want you to be depressed. There is life after death. Look at me. You will do all the things I am doing, and you will do them even better." As I said this, I thought, This is a lie, but some lies are permissible, under certain circumstances.

I find it interesting that I recall the phrase from my conversation with Mario as "life after death," because I don't believe it's entirely accurate. At first, after I lost to Dinkins, I used the term "life after politics" when discussing these issues. I don't know when I made the slight change in my thinking, or why, but there's no question that when you lose a major race in public life it is a form of death. There's no question that when it happens, there is a kind of mourning. You feel a certain kind of depression. You can't help but wonder how you will fill your days. I don't mean to suggest that losing to David Dinkins had no impact on me, because it did. I definitely sought to control its impact, and use it to my advantage, but it left its mark. It left me feeling . . .

well, bewildered. I kept wondering how the good people of New York could have voted me out of office after the good job I had done. I took it personally.

In 1981, when I was completing my first term and running for reelection, I would say, day after day at campaign rallies, "If all the people I have alienated were to go to the polls, you could throw me out. If you do, I'll get a better job, and you won't get a better mayor."

In 1989, I knew I wasn't voted out just for racial reasons. Dinkins was black and I was white, and naturally there were a great many blacks who voted for Dinkins simply because they wanted to put a black mayor in office for the first time in the city's history. This was understandable. I could also appreciate the fact that twelve years is a long time, and I may have worn out my welcome with many voters. But what I couldn't understand (and what I could not at first accept) were the voters who made an effort to distinguish between my record and David Dinkins's, who judged each of us on our merits, and still pulled the lever for my opponent. Especially the Jews! I always laugh about the Jewish vote in New York City, because I always did better with the Catholics — the Irish and the Italians. Typically, among Jews, I pulled about 73 percent of the vote, while the Italians and the Irish voted about 80 percent in my favor. But in the 1989 primary I managed only 65 percent among Jewish voters. This I will never understand, and will never forget.

People are funny. With time, the people who voted me out of office were the same people urging me to run again. Honestly, judging from the tone and tenor of the comments I heard in 1993, when Dinkins was running for a second term, all those who had voted for Dinkins and against me had inexplicably left town. Ten, maybe fifteen times a day, I'd hear shouts of "We miss you, Mayor!" "You must run again, Mayor!" "We made a mistake!" I couldn't leave my apartment, or my office, without hearing that I should run again. Cynics would say that these people were just being nice. They'd counter with "Well, what else are you going to say when you run into the former mayor?" I suppose there was some of that, but beneath the politesse there was also real frustration with the way things were going in the city. The people were very unhappy with David Dinkins, and it wasn't hard to see why. I'd campaigned for him in 1989, against Rudolph Giuliani in the general election, but I believe Dinkins concluded that his greatest contribution to city politics was simply being elected as the first black mayor. After that, he didn't seem to care about the job. He'd never been a particularly hard worker, but he destroyed himself as a public official with his failure to act decisively when a black mob ran riot and engaged in a three-day pogrom against the Lubavitcher Chassidic community in Crown Heights, Brooklyn, killing a young Australian, Yankel Rosenbaum, injuring eighty Jews, and damaging or looting hundreds of Jewish-owned properties. Dinkins's indecisiveness, his failure to take charge, nearly destroyed the city.

But it wasn't just lack of policy or ineffectiveness that did Dinkins in. It was bad judgment. He seemed to make one bad public relations decision after another. I could never understand why Dinkins had a staff member carry his suit jacket on a hanger while he wore an informal nylon jacket on the way to public gatherings, then on arrival put on the suit jacket. It was absolutely silly. I like David Dinkins as a person, and I'm very appreciative that he hasn't gotten mad when I say these kinds of things about him. I've said them all over town, but I like to tell the truth, and with Dinkins the truth (as I saw it) was that he was not up to the job. Or, to give him the benefit of the doubt, perhaps he miscalculated what it would take to do the job well.

Soon enough, I had a ready response to these well-meaning entreaties from people on the street. I can still recall the first time I used it. It was right outside my law office, on Sixth Avenue, sometime in the late winter of 1993. I was heading out to lunch with my good friend Dan Wolf, the onetime *Village Voice* editor and then a member of my staff — one of the "geniuses" I surrounded myself with. We were approached by a middle-aged woman who said, "Mayor, you must run again."

"No," I said back, without a thought. "The people threw me out, and now the people must suffer."

The woman laughed, and Dan and I continued on our way. But then, ever the editor, he said, "A better line would be 'And now the people must be punished.' "

And he was absolutely right. I know a good tag line when I hear one — remember, I'm the guy who came up with the motto "How'm I doin'?" and got such terrific mileage out of it — and here we'd stumbled on a beauty. It's a smart-ass remark, but like most smart-ass remarks with currency and bite a kernel of truth it has, and before long I was finding opportunities to use it several times a day. It's still in my arsenal of retorts — and I'm never wanting for opportunities to use it. There isn't a day that goes by that somebody doesn't say to me, "Oh, you were a great mayor" or words to that effect. Once a man in his forties came up to me and said, "My father thinks you're just absolutely wonderful." I responded, "That's nice, but how about you?" He replied with a smile, "Me, too."

But I knew I'd never run again. I knew that many of these same people who were flagging me down on the street to tell me how wonderful I was would turn on me in a New York minute the moment I announced I was a candidate. That's politics. Right now, I'm a public figure, but not a politician. I'm not a threat or any kind of target. What people remember are the nostalgic aspects of my administration. They remember the good things. They don't remember being tired of seeing me on the six o'clock news every night. They don't remember dis-agreeing with me on some matter or other. Still, I relish these exchanges. I mean, if you were the chairman of IBM during its heyday, and if people on the street remem-bered your name ten years after you retired (which they don't!), wouldn't you love it? Of course you would. It's nice to be remembered. It's nice to be validated. And, most of all, it's nice to be relevant.

This last, for me, is key — as I suspect it is for most of you as well. Remaining relevant has become the central focus of my life since I left office — and I'll gladly be the poster boy for keeping active and vibrant into what has traditionally been known as our retirement years. I may take several medications, and I may exercise daily and watch what I eat, but it's relevance that keeps me young. It's knowing that I still have something to contribute, that my opinions count for something, that my expertise and store of knowledge can be put to meaningful use. We all need to matter, in our own way, and in mine I matter by standing up and being counted. I matter by weighing in with my opinion and knowing that others, even in some small way, might formulate their own opinions based on mine.

I don't remember thinking things through in just this way, when I faced the prospect of life after the mayoralty — but that's how it's been, almost from the very beginning. I can even recall the moment I began considering so-called retirement in these terms, nearly four years after my primary defeat. Like many New Yorkers, I had soured on David

36

Dinkins during his first term in office, and when the 1993 election came around I was ready for a change. And the city was ready for a change. Rudy Giuliani, who lost to Dinkins in the general election in 1989, was back again for another try, and this time around I gave him my endorsement. He importuned me over several lunches — and it helped that he had David Garth in his corner as his media guru. Plus, I thought the city would be destroyed if we had to live through a second Dinkins term.

I don't think Giuliani could have been elected without my support in 1993. I believe there were four people he needed to help ensure his election, and he's even acknowledged my essential participation on several occasions after the election. The first among the essential was the brilliant David Garth, his campaign chairman, and David did a wonderful job. The second was Ray Harding, who delivered the Liberal Party line. The third was Robert Wagner, who did a terrific campaign commercial that gave Democrats a reason to vote for a Republican and not fear their hands would fall off pulling the lever in the voting booth. There are always those "yellow dog" Democrats, so known because they would vote for a yellow dog over a Republican. That's a

Texas phrase, but it flies everywhere, and Giuliani desperately needed to win those people over if he hoped to beat Dinkins. (In 1977, when I was elected, the Republican candidate, Roy Goodman, got 5 percent of the vote in the general election, with Republicans counting for about 20 percent of the city's electorate.) And, finally, he needed me. My popularity had soared since I left office, and as a result of my various roles as a political columnist, talk show host, and all-around public gadfly, my opinions seemed to carry a lot of weight with many New Yorkers. Certainly, as a prominent Democrat, I was uniquely positioned to sway a lot of voters in the '93 election. Mind you, I don't think my endorsement is always so meaningful, but in this particular case it was important. I think everyone involved would agree with that.

Naturally, it wouldn't do for me simply to pull the lever for Giuliani without campaigning for him, so I agreed to hold a press conference to announce my support. We held it right in the conference room at my law office, at Robinson Silverman Pearce Aronsohn & Berman. There were four or five TV cameras present, and a few print reporters. It wasn't the same kind of turnout I'd get when I was still in office, but it was significant. The opening question, with the lights on and the cameras whirring, was, "Mayor, how do you feel at this moment?"

I thought about it, and then I looked heavenward and smiled. "Ah, to be sixty-eight and still relevant," I said.

The line got a good-sized laugh, but it really summed up what I was feeling, and crystallized for me what I wanted to feel going forward. There I was, four years out of office, and still relevant. Let me tell you, it was a wonderful, validating feeling to know your opinion still mattered, to know that you still counted, and I vowed never to lose that heady feeling.

From that day forward, I've worked assiduously to keep myself out in front on issues of local, national, and international importance. I read five newspapers a day and keep abreast of goings-on in City Hall, in Albany, and on Capitol Hill. I study matters of foreign policy and diplomacy the way some New Yorkers study a subway map, especially on issues relating to Israel. I continually consult with a close network of friends and advisers, in and out of government, at home and abroad. And, perhaps most important, I maintain a constant correspondence with leading politicians, businessmen, policy advocates, and opinionmakers — to the point where, I'm sure, some of these people have started to dread a piece of mail with my return address on the envelope. I'll write a letter to anyone — from Yasir Arafat to Secretary of State Madeleine Albright — on any matter that interests me, and if I don't get a response within a reasonable period of time I'll write again. Eventually, I hear back from almost everybody, usually with a substantive reply. It's not always a response to my liking, but that's not the point. The point is I have focused their attention, even if just for a moment, on a matter that I deem important.

Are my experiences germane to a general audience? I believe they are. I realize most people don't have the opportunities available to me. They're not being asked to become partners in a law firm at age sixty-five. They're not hosting talk shows, or lecturing at New York University or Brandeis University, or endorsing Ultra SlimFast, or writing movie reviews. They're not writing a weekly political column for the *Daily News* or being asked to do a movie cameo. But that doesn't mean they can't find ways to keep their hand in, to keep active. Whatever it is you've done in your career, there are ways you can sustain your involvement when you're no longer at it full time. It doesn't have to involve money. Many older people have planned wisely for their retirement years, and the only budget they're concerned with is budgeting their time so they can fill their hours in a meaningful way. For other seniors, the need for supplemental income often informs the choices they must make when they leave the job or career that provided their principal livelihood.

I also believe that, just as winning is better than losing, getting paid is better than *pro bono,* even though, in my case, money has never been the main issue. I've been lucky. Right now, I happen to be making a lot of money, but if I never earn another dollar I can still live comfortably for the rest of my life.

I'm always looking for something productive to do, and compensation rarely enters into the equation when I think about signing on. I don't ever want to be taken advantage of, but money is rarely the deciding factor. All those years in public office, in Congress or in City Hall, I didn't make a lot of money, so I believe I'm entitled to be finally making some now, even though my lifestyle doesn't require a lot of it. I have fairly modest needs, and those needs were clearly being met back when I was a public official, before the people threw me out. But

I'd keep the same schedule, and work just as hard, even if there was no money involved in these new careers of mine. It's the way I've always been, and the way I'll always be.

What follows, then, is a look at how I've managed to remain relevant since leaving office, and how my extra efforts have kept me feeling vital and — dare I say it? — young. The secret, I insist, is keeping current, keeping active, keeping one step ahead of the curve. I am constantly working. I half-expect (and fully hope) to die at my desk, or at the microphone, somewhere on the job. I made a pact with God, back in 1987 when I had my stroke, back when I was mayor. I said, "God, I'm not afraid to die, but take me all at once, or not at all. No salami tactics." So far, He's kept His word, and I mean to make the most of it. My commitment is to fight injustice and to take on the public bullies. I mean to keep busy at the work I've always loved, to continue to exploit the late-in-life talents I've developed, and to follow up new opportunities.

As the title of this book emphatically states, I'm not done yet! And I don't plan on being done anytime soon.

Two

A Place to Go

I've tried never to live in the past. I suppose this is a learned trait, and I suppose I learned it from my parents, Louis Koch and Yetta Silpe, two Polish-Jewish immigrants born in the Austro-Hungarian Empire who didn't have much to look back on. (My mother later Americanized her first name and called herself Joyce.) Indeed, at times in their young lives, it might have appeared there wasn't all that much for my parents to look forward to, but somehow they persevered and managed to build a family together. That they did so, I believe, was a tribute to their strength of character and resolve.

That strength flowed directly from their childhood, and their circumstances. My parents were from a part of Poland that is now in Ukraine. According to my father, who came to America at the age of fourteen, Poland was a place to suffer. Everyone suffered, he said, but particularly the Jews. Truly, from the stories he used to tell, he had a difficult childhood — and yet, were it not for his unique experiences he would have been different, perhaps less strong in character and physical toughness, and it's possible his children would have been diminished in these areas as well, since we all learn by example. As a small boy, he worked with his father as a peddler, trading manufactured goods from a horse-drawn wagon for the agricultural wares of the local peasants. It was hard work, with no time off for normal childhood pursuits, and my father never forgot it. Years later, when my then eight-year-old nephew Jared asked him what he did for fun, he said, "In the winter, we would go inside to get warm."

My mother also came to this country at fourteen, and her childhood was no less harsh. It was clear to her very early on that any opportunity for a better life would come in America, and she held out the prospect like a dream. As in most families, the oldest child would emigrate first to America, and then bring over the next one, and so it was in my mother's family. Once in America, however, she was treated like a servant by her older brother, Louis, who put her to work in a grocery store he owned, and in his home taking care of his children. Still, she made the best of what she had. She had no formal education, but she managed to make her way through a women's-wear design school and eventually became quite a good blouse designer, according to what I've been told by relatives.

My mother was highly intelligent, and a wonderful administrator of family affairs, operating a household budget of modest means with superb ability and maximum efficiency. My father had a gentle personality, very compassionate, and he was truly loved by those whom he worked with and befriended. He was not as smart as my mother, however, and their life together as husband and wife was filled with arguments. My mother believed Papa never rose to the success she had hoped to have with him. Had they been born later in the century, I'm sure they ultimately would have divorced. Instead, they lived out their lives together without ever finding true marital happiness — and doing so, as I heard my mother say many times, "for the sake of the children."

Their personalities undoubtedly molded the characters of their three children — my brother Harold, myself, and my sister Pat. We learned early on to cope with life and its challenges. We lived with reality, never fantasy. Even now, after I have achieved a great deal of financial success, I still emphasize reality. I rarely, if ever, fantasize outcomes.

In addition to never-ending drive and ambition, I also inherited a sense of humor from my father, and a sense of perspective from my mother. They had these traits in abundance. They also had tempers, which they passed on to me as well. However, unlike them, I've been able to harness my temper. I try not to display my anger through heat and yelling; rather, I display indifference, making sure the offending party ultimately understands my anger through my detached coolness. Like my father, I hold a grudge, but unlike my father, I always remember the infraction. He was forever not speaking to some relative or other, but not entirely sure why. Some of us can recall the punishment better than the offense — but I remember both.

What I find most compelling now, considering the themes to be discussed in these pages, is not how my parents lived but how they died. Or, to put a finer point on it, what resonates is how they aged, and how they faced the later years of their lives. My mother died of cancer at the age of sixty-two, in 1960. Today, she would have been considered a young woman, but at the time she seemed very old to me. Certainly, the cancer contributed mightily to her elderly and frail appearance, but I remember her as "old" even before she took ill. She was old in her walk, old in her thinking, old in the way she approached each day. I don't mean she was old-fashioned, but from the time I was a young man, she carried her years like a burden. She just seemed elderly — and she had been a beautiful woman in her youth. My father, too, seemed older than his years, although to a much lesser degree. He never lost his desire to work. He did live to become chronologically old, dying at eighty-seven, and in his case thankfully he did not suffer, dying immediately of a heart attack, but he was relatively active and free of pain until the very end.

Sadly, my father lacked the education that might have made his later years more meaningful for him, and I've often wondered how different his life might have been had he been involved in some meaningful intellectual pursuit. Instead, he retired to Florida, far too soon to suit him, and against his own desires, as I shall relate.

His eyes gave him away, toward the end of

his life. His eyesight wasn't failing him, but he had the beginnings of the vacant and teary eye you sometimes see in older people when there's no longer much of substance going on in their day-to-day lives. Do you know that look? There's no vital life force behind the eyes. There's not much happening. There's no *there* there. The eyes are looking at you or, more accurately, right through you, but they aren't really registering. And when you see that emptiness in the eyes of someone you love, it's very painful.

My father never meant to retire. He tried it once, at about the age I am now, and it took only six months or so before he regretted it. Actually, I think he regretted it right away, but it took six months for the regret to bubble forth. Let me tell you the story. About a year after my mother's death, my father remarried. She was a kind but intellectually limited woman named Rose, a widow, and they lived together in her apartment up in the Bronx. (Indeed, she owned the apartment building in which they resided.) He had been, for most of my adult life, a small, modestly successful fur coat manufacturer. He had worked at a variety of jobs throughout my childhood, most memorably for my uncle in the hat check concession in Kruger's Auditorium in Newark, New Jersey, during the Depression years of 1931–1941, but the work that ultimately defined him was as a furrier. He partnered with a nice man named Eddie Goldstein, and they called their business — what else? — Koch & Goldstein, although by the middle 1960s it wasn't much of a business. It was a place to go to every morning, and busy themselves for the day, eking out a bare living.

This situation didn't sit well with Papa's new wife. Rose's first husband had left her comfortably situated. My father continued to work, but his income was very modest. He worked, and he worked, and it didn't seem to make a difference. Some time after he remarried, his new wife said to him, "Louie, I want you to stop working. It's not nice for the neighbors, that you work at your age."

My father liked working. He wanted to work. He'd worked all his life. For a long time, during the Depression, he had two jobs, simply to get by: checking hats and coats at night and working at odd jobs in what remained of the fur trade in New York throughout the day. To me, it was always incredible that he was able to support a family on what he made. I think it had to do with the fact that my mother was such a good manager. In Yiddish, the term is *baleboosteh*. It means, simply, a manager, and boy, could she manage! In the early 1940s, my father was bringing home $65 a week, and my mother was raising three children, and *managing*. He always had his own little business, but he never made much. I once said to him, "Papa, how can you stay in business? You tell us every year you're losing money." And he said, "Sonny, we make it up in inventory."

Ah, the joy of a Jewish sense of humor! *We will survive!*

Anyway, at this late stage in his life he was still leaving the house at five o'clock in the morning and making his way to the fur district, at Thirtieth Street and Seventh Avenue, and sitting with his friends at the local cafeteria, the Bake Oven. This was his routine. I used to go to the Bake Oven myself every once in a while, before I became mayor, when I occasionally visited him at his fur loft. It was something for him to look forward to, every morning. He would go and be with his friends. It got him out of the house. When Rose made her feelings about not working known to him, he was just about the age I am now, in his early to middle seventies. She didn't like being alone during the day, or being tied to New York. She wanted to spend time in Florida during the winter months.

So he came to us one day — "us" being my sister Pat, my brother Harold, and me — and he asked for our advice. She's threatening to leave me, he said, and go to Florida by herself. He believed she meant it.

Papa, we told him, given the circumstances, we think you should stop work. You care about this woman, and she cares about you, and if this is important to her then it's something you should do. The business was not a moneymaker. None of us wanted to see him give up work, but even more than that none of us wanted Rose to leave him. Underneath that admission was the somewhat more complex truth that none of us wanted him to move in with us. Of course, if necessary, each of us would have taken him in because we loved him, but we were hoping we wouldn't have to. More accurately put, we were praying.

And so Papa sold out his share of the business to his partner and tried for six months to make a go of retirement.

I was a congressman at the time, and spending most of my days in Washington, dreading the reports I would hear from my brother and sister on my father's depressed state of mind. He was climbing the walls, he was so bored. Finally, my father called me at my congressional office in Washington, to tell me how miserable he was, and what he hoped I could help him do about it. "Eddie," he said, "I'm so bored. I've made a terrible mistake. You've got to help me. You've got to get me a job."

"Papa," I said, "I don't have any jobs."

He said, "Yes, you do." He was adamant, like I was holding something back.

I said, "Papa, honest. I don't have any jobs."

"You could get me a job at the post office," he insisted.

I said, "Papa, if I got you a job in the post office, I'd go to jail."

He paused to consider this. "Well," he finally said, "then you could get me a job at OTB," meaning in one of the off-track betting stations around the city.

"Papa," I laughed. "I'd rather go to jail than call Howard Samuels and ask him for a favor." Howard Samuels was the head of OTB, not a special friend of mine, and certainly not a man I wanted to be indebted to, for any reason. Indeed, I supported Congressman Hugh Carey over him when they both ran in the Democratic primary for governor of New York.

My father was very upset with me, and I couldn't stop thinking about his anguish, so I shared this story with my administrative assistant, Ronay Arlt, who would stay with me throughout my congressional and mayoral career. "Ronay," I said, "I don't know what to do. I feel so badly for him. I want to help him." I wasn't the kind of congressman who could trade political favors for jobs, but I loved my father and understood his agony.

Ronay understood my dilemma, as she uniquely managed to understand every one of my dilemmas throughout my political career, and said she would see what she could do. She knew a lot of people. She knew someone at Bloomingdale's, and she arranged an interview for my father at the fur storage department, which I thought was wonderful. Why hadn't I thought of that? And do you know what happened? They hired him, to work in their summer storage vault. The only drawback to the job was that my father couldn't write in English, other than his name. He was a reasonably smart man, but he had lived in Poland until he was a teenager. He could read, write, and speak Polish and Yiddish, and he learned to speak and read English, but he was never able to write it. He never went to school in this country. And even when he wrote his name, you had to already know that it was his name to decipher the letters. But you're allowed to write your name any way you want to in this country. It's yours.

Nevertheless, my father was a resourceful man. He found a brilliant way to deal with the problem. An East Side *grande dame* would come in to store her coat for the summer, and he would say to her, "Would you please fill out this card?" And he would hand her the card, with all the information the store needed to complete the transaction. After the customer presented her name and address, he would invariably say, "I see by your address that my son is your congressman."

It didn't make any difference if the person lived in Alaska. It was his standard line. The customer would usually respond, "Who is your son?" And my father would proudly say, "Ed Koch." At that point, the customer would usually say something along the lines of "Oh, he's wonderful." Whether she meant it or not was unimportant because my father felt like a million bucks each time it happened, and apparently it happened quite often.

He stayed at Bloomingdale's for several years, full time, and I firmly believe it kept him younger. He was happy. He had a salary. His customers and his fellow employees all came to love him. He had a reason to get up in the morning, and a place to go. He *mattered.* I still meet people who remember him fondly from his days at Bloomingdale's. And I always look back on that period in my father's life with great fondness, as well — and with gratitude, because without meaning to, the management at Bloomingdale's gave him a tremendous gift. In their minds, they just hired someone to do a job that needed doing, but in mine they gave my father a second chance. They gave him back his routine, his place to go. They kept my father feeling relevant, and alive.

But even Bloomingdale's couldn't stop the clock and keep my father from retiring a second time. After several years, Rose prevailed upon him once again to quit his job, and this time there was no turning back. This time, he fully (though fitfully) retired — to Florida, where he lived in air-conditioned comfort in one of the Jewish condominium complexes in Fort Lauderdale. I then made a promise to myself. I would never retire. I knew the day would come when I would not hold public office, but retirement? I saw how it ate at my father, and I knew it wouldn't sit well with me. I was proud of my father, for correcting his error on the first pass and returning to work. It was a brave, ennobling thing to start over, in a new job, as an older man. It could not have been easy. And he even proved to be an asset to Bloomingdale's fur department. Good for him, I always thought. Good for Bloomingdale's. And good for me, to have that picture of my own father, working even tangentially at the only business he had ever truly known, even after he had first thought to give it up.

But I knew I could never retire. The more I thought about it — particularly when it became clear I would not be elected to a fourth term as mayor — the more I realized I could never walk away from meaningful, purposeful work. That my father did so a second time, after several years at Bloomingdale's, doesn't in any way diminish the life he lived or the choices he made. It's just that I couldn't make the same choices for myself. Retirement eventually suited his purposes, even as I realized it would not suit mine. I would not move to Florida, or to some warmer, more forgiving (and, certainly, more sterile) environment, as so many of my friends, colleagues, and relatives seemed to be doing with each passing year. I would not go gently into my twilight years.

But how would I fill my days, once I'd left what had been the central passion of my life? From 1969 to 1989, I had worked only in public office. It had been my one true profession. I was so far removed from the practice of law, which I left when I was elected to Congress, that I didn't think I would ever go back to being a lawyer. What would I do? How would I remain relevant, and purposeful, and active?

Here's what I did. I sat down with Allen Schwartz, my former law partner and one-time corporation counsel, who at that time was himself back at the practice of law. He was subsequently appointed federal district court judge for the Southern District of New York, a position he currently holds. Allen was, and remains, a tremendous sounding board for me. I've solicited his advice on every important personal decision I've had to make since we first met. As a matter of fact, it was over lunch one day in 1964, at the single desk we shared in our law office of Koch & Schwartz at 52 Wall Street, that I first articulated my intention to run for mayor. As Allen remembered it, I greeted the arrival of his first child, David, with the following comment: "When I become mayor, David can be bar mitzvahed at Gracie Mansion." Just to finish the story,

Allen reminded me of my promise soon after I was sworn in, after he had begun working as my corporation counsel. He didn't have to. I remembered, and as far as I know David Schwartz was the first boy to become bar mitzvahed in Gracie Mansion. (Not to be outdone, my brother Harold asked that his stepdaughter, Joey, be bat mitzvahed in the mansion's Susan E. Wagner Wing, and she became the first girl to be so honored.)

Allen came to my office one day in the fall of 1989, not long after I was defeated in the Democratic primary, and said, "We're gonna sit down, and we're gonna figure out your next move."

It was, I thought, a practical, thorough-going approach to what had quickly become a growing concern for everyone around me, and I believe it's a key step for anyone going through a major transition in life. It's one thing to think about what it is you'd like to do when you're forced to make a major professional change, but it's quite another to sit down with a good and trusted (and savvy) friend who can help evaluate and guide your options. It's the difference between a passive approach and an active one, and I was never one to sit back and let good things come to me. I still had a few months remaining in my term, but I wanted to hit the ground running, so we kicked around some ideas. In our conversation, we kept coming back to the law. It was a logical next step, although if you had asked me I might have told you I never expected to go back to the practice of law. Even so, I knew that the law itself would not make me happy. There would have to be other activities to consume my energy, interests, and talents as well.

Allen pointed out, quite reasonably, that I would need some sort of home base for what would hopefully become an assortment of opportunities, and that a law firm would be a good place to start. We both realized I would never be expected to litigate or become an expert again in any special field. I wasn't about to learn of all the changes that had taken place since I gave up the practice of law to become a congressman. In the early days of my political career, you didn't have to give up your practice upon election the way you do today, but I never believed you could be a full-time public official, at any level, and still maintain a career as an attorney. There are too many conflicts, in terms of both your time and your interests, and so I voluntarily terminated my ties to my law firm, which was then known as Koch, Lankenau, Schwartz & Kovner. I am very proud of the fact that ours is the only law firm in the history of the city to produce one mayor and two corporation counsels; Victor Kovner became corporation counsel in David Dinkins's administration.

My value to any firm would be to bring in clients and open doors, since I knew so many people in and out of government. I had no hopes of being a traditional "rainmaker," bringing in lots of new clients. I didn't hang around with rich people, with a few exceptions, and those few I knew well were not in need of my services as a lawyer and would not be hiring me. I would become involved in any ongoing projects where it was felt my contacts or expertise in city matters was needed, and although I knew I would never engage in lobbying, I would certainly work to advance our clients' interests, if I believed in them. I would also be generally available to colleagues and clients interested in meeting me. In sum, I would be a kind of goodwill ambassador for the firm in general, and provide strategic and tactical advice, particularly to those seeking to do business with the city.

This, Allen pointed out, would be a worthwhile contribution to any of a number of top law firms in the city. He had even scoped out interest at his old firm,

Proskauer Rose. Their chairman, Ed Silver, had served my administration as a labor consultant, advising our in-house labor relations commissioner, and he did a very, very good job, and if he wanted me on board I would have to consider it very seriously. The understanding was that I would be allowed, even encouraged, to pursue other areas of interest — which would include television and radio commentary, as well as commercial endorsements and speaking engagements — and that I would not be called upon to fill out time sheets for the firm.

We very quickly reached an agreement on terms, but then something extraordinary happened, and for this next turn of events I will always be grateful to God. I happen to believe in God, so . . . Thanks, God. Here's what happened. Allen told our mutual friend Jim Gill, a senior partner in the prestigious midtown law firm of Robinson Silverman Pearce Aronsohn & Berman, that I was looking for a partnership. Allen and Jim had served in the district attorney's office under Frank Hogan, and they remained close friends. When I was mayor, Allen recommended Jim for an ad-hoc chairmanship investigating corruption in the public schools, which he handled superbly. So we had a history together, and he called me up and told me he knew I was casting about for my next move and suggested there might be a good fit at Robinson Silverman.

I said, "Well, Jim, I don't know. I've already told Ed Silver that I would accept his offer, and I'd like to keep my word to him."

"I understand," Jim said. "All I want is for the two of us to have lunch and we'll sit down and talk about it. We'll have Chinese."

Jim knew me well enough to know that Chinese food was an addiction for me. The thrust of Jim's pitch was that Robinson Silverman was a small, friendly place. At the time, he was looking to make me the firm's forty-third partner. There are many more partners at Robinson Silverman today, but at that time Proskauer Rose was a much larger firm. "But it's not just the size that will make you feel more comfortable," Jim said. "It's the culture of the firm you'll appreciate. Everyone knows one another here. You will be more than just a partner. You'll be a friend."

And do you know what? He's been absolutely right, in every respect. Of course, I couldn't know this going in, but I trusted Jim and he told me things would be different at his firm. Lord knows, if I'd gone with a really large firm, and if business soured, I'd be one of the first to go in any kind of downsizing because I was never going to bring in a massive number of new clients. But we don't get rid of people at Robinson Silverman because of economics; as Jim suggested, we are truly a firm with a special culture. To illustrate, during the downsizing that took place throughout the city's law firms, beginning with the recession that hit the region in the early 1990s, Robinson Silverman didn't ask a single partner to leave. I look at my colleagues as friends, and they look at me in the same way.

When I called Ed Silver to tell him I wouldn't be joining his firm after all, he immediately thought it was about money. He didn't come right out and say he'd match whatever Robinson Silverman was paying me, but in fact that wasn't necessary — Robinson Silverman had already matched Ed's initial offer to me. I told him that it wasn't about money. It was difficult to explain my decision without insulting him, but I tried. I knew Jim Gill's firm was the right environment for me, and as things have turned out I was right. Had I gone anywhere else, I would have been miserable.

And so I took the job at Robinson Silverman and thought back to my father, signing on at Bloomingdale's fur department, all those years earlier. There was never any doubt that I would strive to find new and worthy challenges after my political career, but I made the connection to what my father must have faced in having to develop a new routine, and in having to find a new place to go. For him, working in the storage vault wasn't the same thing as having his own fur business, but it was close enough. For me, working as a partner in a midtown law firm was certainly not the same as being mayor of the greatest city in the world. It wasn't even the same as being a congressman representing 520,000 people in the greatest city in the world, but it had its own important and interesting challenges.

I had my place to go. Now all I had to do was figure out what I'd do when I got there.

Three

Moving Forward

I commenced my new life, confident that I would contribute in some meaningful ways to the firm, but unsure what form those contributions might take.

As it shook out, I was not any kind of "rainmaker," although my partners say that I have added enormously to the firm's recognition and prominence. I am always available to consult on matters relating to city government or ordinances, and to meet with prospective clients of other partners. I decorated my new law office with some wonderful pictures and other mementos from my three terms as mayor, and it became part of the routine for Robinson Silverman clients to stop by to say hello and have a look around.

In addition to finding my way in the corporate culture, I began to explore some of the personal opportunities that were presenting themselves, and the first of these was decidedly personal in nature. It involved an issue that had been a concern of mine for most of my adult life: my weight. I'd put on a few too many pounds during my three terms as mayor — forty, to be exact. I'm told that most people gain an average of three pounds each year, if they maintain the same diet and lifestyle. Strangely, as the body ages it becomes more efficient in the use of food to provide energy, and I'm told that this "efficiency" yields an excess of fat. You have to watch what you eat at any age, but the older you get the more you have to exercise to keep those annual weight gains to a minimum, and as mayor I found it difficult to do either of those things. With all the public luncheons and dinners I was asked to attend, and with all the wonderful food that invariably turned up at such functions (served in what I soon recognized as mayoral portions), it was really tough. Given the circumstances, forty pounds in twelve years wasn't all that bad, but it wasn't how I wanted to look going forward. It wasn't good for me. It wasn't the way I saw myself. To my mind, there was always a thin guy inside of me, seeking to be liberated.

I managed to lose the weight through the Ultra SlimFast diet program, primarily as the result of an enormous incentive: They hired me as their spokesperson. On my own, simply using portion control or skipping a meal now and then, I don't think I ever could have done it. I am, by nature, a fairly disciplined person, but for some reason that discipline goes out the window when it comes to diet and exercise. I enjoy good food too much to deny myself for very long, and early on I recognized I wasn't cut out to be a jock — and that includes *all* forms of exercise.

Happily, the folks at SlimFast provided me with the kind of discipline I couldn't provide myself. They thought I could help them connect with a more adult, more sedentary audience than they'd been reaching with their previous commercials. The SlimFast representatives actually contacted me when I lost the primary, and we got together soon after I left office to discuss terms.

We think you'd be terrific, they said.

I thought so, too.

SlimFast offered me a huge sum of money to lose thirty pounds in a fixed period of time. I was aware that the company had hired Los Angeles Dodgers manager Tommy Lasorda for a similar campaign, and I didn't like the idea of a former mayor receiving less than a former baseball player, so I told them I wanted whatever he was making.

They very quickly agreed, and then I added, "What will you pay for forty pounds?"

They thought about it, they added 25 percent to their offer, and we were in business. Let me tell you, it was a painless way to lose the weight — and surprisingly effective. The program required me to drink a SlimFast shake for breakfast and another for lunch, and allowed me to eat a sensible, balanced meal each night at dinner, and in five months and eleven days the forty pounds were gone. It also reinforced for me a valuable lesson: Never give up. I'd always found it nearly impossible to lose weight for health reasons, but now I know it can be done. To you, the reader, I offer the same message: Never give up. Being overweight is the greatest danger to our health, especially as we age. It is never too late to do something about it.

I finally did do something, and for the first time in a long time I felt terrific. I also felt good about my opportunities, which began to take shape in those first few months. My days were once again full. Or, I should say, they remained full. There was never any real drop-off, from the moment I left City Hall to the moment I moved into my new office in midtown Manhattan. Mind you, my days weren't yet filled with the kind of consequential, all-consuming matters that had filled my days as mayor, but I realized it would take some time to find my new way. A part of that new way, I felt sure, would come through my writing — either in book form, or in newspaper commentary — but before I could put pen to paper on any kind of sustained project, I was redirected by a chance meeting. That the meeting took place in the same excellent Italian restaurant on Third Avenue — Parma — where I passed out one night as mayor (a result, I believe, of three of us drinking four bottles of wine in about two hours) reinforced for me the idea that you can sometimes stumble across good fortune and misfortune at the same place. This time, the evening was a little less alarming, but no less momentous. A man sitting at the next table leaned over, introduced himself as Michael Kakoyiannis, and offered me a spot doing morning radio commentary on WNEW-AM, a popular New York station.

He wanted to team me with two disc jockeys named Rosenberg and Fitz. On the one hand, it was the same kind of natural fit that had found my father some years earlier at Bloomingdale's — the chance to trade on my earlier experiences in another, not unrelated field — but on the other, it interfered with my gym schedule. My Greek god–like appearance was owed to a little more than SlimFast, and I had gotten into the good habit of rising early each morning and being in the gym by 6:15. It was a good habit I wasn't prepared to break. The situation Kakoyiannis proposed would have had me tied to a studio at 7:30 each morning, and thrown my barely established workout schedule out the window. I wasn't inclined to give up the routine for a five-minute local radio spot, but thanked him just the same.

Kakoyiannis was not to be put off. He suggested that we tape the commentary each morning from my apartment, by telephone, before I left for the gym. Wonderful! I thought, whereupon I jumped at the offer. My WNEW contract paid $25,000 in the first year, which wasn't bad for five minutes' work, five days a week. And it wasn't a bad way to announce my arrival in New York City as a kind of commentator/gadfly/god-about-town. Plus, I was an experienced radio hand. I'm sure Kakoyiannis had no idea, but back in the early 1970s, as a congressman, I hosted a fifteen-minute weekly show for WNYC-AM, which I recorded in Washington in the congressional radio studio. The reason I was so sure Kakoyiannis had no idea was that I didn't have too many listeners. I never got any mail at the station. We never measured our ratings. (Or maybe we did and never managed to crack the scale.) Once, just to assure myself that I wasn't broadcasting into some black hole, I asked my hoped-for WNYC listeners to write in and offer some validation for our efforts. In exchange, as an enticement, I promised to send back my recipe for shrimp jambalaya. As it happened, I could no more cook a meal of shrimp jambalaya than I could open my own restaurant, but I was desperate and it seemed like a good idea at the time. It sounded like just the sort of exotic, out-there promotion to generate response. And it did. I got one letter from a listener — just one! — and I made good on my pledge by asking a congressional colleague from New Orleans for his family recipe.

As a veteran broadcaster, then, I was all but certain I would attract a few more listeners to WNEW than I could to WNYC.

After all, now I was a *name* talent. (See how I picked up on all the right phrases?) Now I had a popular morning slot, sharing time and swapping opinions with two disc jockeys with opposing points of view. It was a good situation, all around, and I made the best of it. Actually, I quite enjoyed the give-and-take on the air, and the chance to vent my spoken opinions in such a public way. I especially enjoyed the almost immediate feedback from listeners. I'd say something from my apartment, in the predawn hours, over the telephone, and just a short time later, on the streets of the city, I'd hear back from someone I'd upset or surprised with my views. It was a tremendously validating experience, and it gave me something like the immediate connection with New Yorkers I enjoyed as mayor.

I always knew I'd gravitate toward some type of commentary work after leaving office, but now that it was upon me I stopped to think how much I enjoyed it. Really, it was liberating, after spending so many years in the bottled-up world of city politics. As mayor, I'd made it a point to implement the motto "The Truth Is Still Relevant," which I kept on my desk. (Incidentally, it was the same desk that Fiorello La Guardia had used. It had long before been taken out of the mayor's office, and was being used by one of the secretaries when I arrived. My predecessor, Abe Beame, had used a replica of George Washington's desk, but I returned La Guardia's desk to the mayor's office, where it rightly belonged.) Back to my motto: I let the people know I wouldn't submit to unreasonable public opinion or political correctness, or to the pressures created by special interests, but there was still a limit on what I would or wouldn't say in response. I would try not to overly offend those in power who could hurt the city if they got really angry at something I said. I didn't really care if they got angry at me, but I did care about protecting the city from their wrath, so I was careful when attacking people like Governor Carey or Felix Rohatyn, as I did from time to time. Now that I was out of office, however, that limitation didn't exist, and I was free to speak my mind without fear of repercussions. What counted, I determined, was to tell the truth, air controversial issues, and seek to educate the listeners. Everything else would just have to take care of itself.

The WNEW spots became known for my freewheeling opinions and no-nonsense style. The fact is they were virtually the same opinions I had always held, but here they were dressed up and delivered with a candor that even I couldn't manage under the constraints of public office. And, by all accounts, the morning reports were wildly popular. In the second year of my contract, I earned $150,000 for the same five-minute spot. There was no third year. The station was sold, as I recall, and I was out of a job I'd very much enjoyed. Truly, I hated to see my radio days come to an end. More than anything else I would do in my postmayoral life, my time on the radio was enormously gratifying — and this taped gig eventually led to an hour-long call-in show on one of New York's most powerful stations that would prove to be even more rewarding.

It's interesting, but almost every opportunity that found me in my postmayoral career was in one way or another the result of losing a previous job — starting, of course, with my mayoral career itself. If New York City Democrats had voted for me in the primary in 1989, I would not have been free to pursue the Robinson Silverman offer. And if WNEW had decided to renew my contract under new ownership, I couldn't have signed on at WABC — a much bigger radio station, which in January 1992 offered me my own call-in show, for a full hour, at 11:00 A.M. each weekday, at a salary that went to $300,000.

I was a little intimidated by the prospect — and the prospect was even more intimidating when it was first pitched to me. Initially, WABC wanted me for a two- or three-hour program, which was more in keeping with the station's format. At the time, most of its shows were scheduled to run at least two hours, but I couldn't see how I would ever fill that amount of time. The jump from five minutes a day, taped, with two cohosts, to two hours a day, live, on my own, was too daunting, so I prevailed upon the station to consider an hour-long format. An hour, I thought I could handle.

The folks at WABC agreed to set up a mini-studio in my law office, so that I wouldn't even have to leave my desk to do the show. That's how accommodating they were, how important it was to them for me to feel comfortable, and they saw to everything. All I had to do, every weekday morning, was swivel my chair around to the console, put on my headset, and start in. And once I started in, there was no turning back. I wondered where this notion of hosting my own radio show had been my entire professional life. I thoroughly enjoyed it. When we started out, I offered my unedited commentary on the news of the day, for about the first ten minutes or so. It was like putting out my own daily newspaper. In preparation, I only had to read the morning newspapers, which I had already done. Of course, I quickly found, you tend to read the newspapers a little bit differently, perhaps more diligently, if you expect to be quoting from them later on, but the arrangement didn't add significantly to my already busy days, since I was an avid newspaper reader. Nevertheless, it kept me focused, and keenly aware of the latest developments in local, national, and international politics.

The routine I established was this: I would read the early editions of the *Times* and the *News* the night before, when they hit the newsstands, and then I'd read the other newspapers delivered early in the morning. I was on the list of people who received the *Times* at 11 P.M., by special courier delivery, arranged by the newspaper for its own people and a few others that publisher Punch Sulzberger added to the list. I asked to be added to the list, and was very appreciative when I was. Punch's successor, his son Arthur, sent me a note that in the interest of economy, a number of people were being pruned from the list, and I was one of them. He hoped I would understand. I certainly did, and I thanked him by note for the generosity of the *Times* in having provided the special delivery all those years. I coped with the change by getting up a little earlier each morning and reading my copy of the *Times* with the other papers that came to my door by a regular commercial service.

After the commentary at the top of the show, I opened the phone lines to our listeners. We never wanted for interesting callers. New York being the colorful place that it is, and talk radio being the colorful outpost of all manner of life forms, there were always some kooks sprinkled in among our more thoughtful listeners, but I even enjoyed the back-and-forth with the people on the fringe. It was a constant challenge to move the show along, so I developed a style that allowed me to keep a tight rein on the proceedings. I got in the habit of saying, "Stop!" when a caller refused to give up the floor, so I could provide my point of view. In the beginning, some thought my manner rude, but I explained that it was my obligation to keep the show interesting, and moving. When a caller was boring, or bigoted, I sometimes ended a call by saying, "Thank you, but you haven't added to my education. Good-bye." Or, "Bye-bye. I don't allow racists or anti-Semites on my program."

Again, some people might have thought me abrupt, but I was merely doing my job in a professional manner, under the circumstances. I found myself struggling, in my first few weeks on the air, to come up with a signature line, some tag or hook that I could use to help fix my new presence on the New York airwaves. I never underestimated the value of a good catchphrase, and here I stumbled across one I would wear for the next seven years. I was asked by the station manager to repeat the call letters WABC before each call, and leading into each commercial break. One day, my partner Jim Gill listened to the program from my office and suggested "Ed Koch, the voice of reason." A new slogan had been born. I started using it right away, whenever I reported the station's call letters. I liked the association. I'd air controversial topics, and let the callers ask their questions, and then I'd weigh in with my final comments and my signature I.D., "Ed Koch, the voice of reason," before moving on to the next call.

The phrase quickly took on its own momentum, to the point where some callers, apparently tired of addressing me as "Ed," or "Mayor," started referring to me as "Voice of Reason." I enjoyed that. I also referred to myself on occasion as "a liberal with sanity," but Voice of Reason connected better with listeners. When some argued with my asserting the right to interrupt them, I usually replied by saying something like "You have an opportunity to speak, but we play by *my* rules of engagement or we don't play." To this, the response was always "Okay, Mayor."

Ultimately, WABC decided not to renew my contract, after seven years, which I took to be a good, long run. Previously, when the station changed hands and was purchased by Disney, my salary had been reduced to $200,000, but I stayed on because I liked the work. My agent told me that the reason WABC canceled the program had to do with the station wanting to expand the time it devoted to two of its popular syndicated programs. It had Dr. Laura Schlessinger on before me, and Rush Limbaugh following me, and WABC didn't like having my regional show sandwiched between these national powerhouses. (In the end, my hour was added to Dr. Laura's program.) It was their station, and they could do whatever they wanted. I left feeling richer for the experience — and I don't mean because of my salary, although I was well paid — and determined to take my act to another New York station. As of this writing, those efforts have not materialized, but I remain hopeful of landing a regular slot at another station; of all my postmayoral jobs, radio is what I enjoyed the most, and what I miss the most, now that I've moved on.

I was busier and busier in those first few years after leaving office, and underneath each new assignment was the unspoken realization that I was quietly succeeding in what I had taken to calling the "third act" of my professional life. First, there was my career as a young attorney, from 1949 to 1969; then there was my political career, culminating in a nine-year run as a United States congressman and a twelve-year stint as mayor of New York City; and now there was my burgeoning career as a somewhat older attorney/product spokesperson/commentator. Soon after leaving the mayoralty, I began doing a Sunday-morning interview program on WCBS-TV Channel 2, the local CBS television station. I must say, I never found the television work as rewarding as radio, but it was a good gig — until I was fired for being too controversial. I should have seen it coming, although if I had, I wouldn't have conducted myself any differently. Television, with its broader ratings base, is much more of a lowest-common-denominator medium. Radio, on the other hand, reaches a far narrower audience, which often allows you to speak more freely.

I wasn't about to change my stripes just because there was a camera pointed at me, and about a year into my Sunday program I criticized New York Congressman Charles Rangel for his reelection endorsement of Illinois Congressman Gus Savage, a well-known anti-Semite, who happens to be black. Rangel, who is also black, tended to receive favorable, hands-off treatment from the mostly white media elite in New York, who were petrified of criticizing him and being called racists, but I wasn't afraid of any such thing. I suppose some might have also worried about unfavorable tax consequences of a public feud, given that Rangel was a ranking member of the House Ways and Means Committee, but I wasn't afraid of this either. In the end, such fearlessness cost me, but at this point it was just one job out of many, which meant it was a price I was willing to pay. Indeed, I couldn't afford *not* to speak my mind — on this or any other issue. My reputation as an independent, uninhibited commentator was far more important to me than any paycheck. WCBS-TV canned me just the same, paying me half of the salary due for the balance of my contract.

After I left WCBS, I joined Channel 5 Fox Television, where I remained from mid-May 1991 until the end of 1995. Fox issued a press release on May 2, 1991, which gave me a sense of pleasure. It reported, "After Koch left WCBS-TV in January 1991 Nielsen ratings for 'Sunday Edition' suffered a 17 percent decline." Ultimately, I terminated my employment with Fox when we could not agree on the terms of a new contract. Television contracts have more ups and downs than a roller-coaster, but they're fun, and after leaving any TV job, I found the next one to be even more rewarding in challenge and salary.

I would soon add to my expanding job description the title of movie reviewer, which in 1991 became the latest unlikely turn in my working days. I took a call from Tom Allon, the editor of a small local weekly called the Manhattan *Spirit*, who had heard I was a big movie fan. This was true. Even as mayor, I had enjoyed going to the movies, and now that I was out of office and my evenings and weekends were largely my own, I enjoyed it even more. Tom wanted to know if I would consider writing a weekly column of movie reviews. I was intrigued.

"How much do you pay?" I asked. Now that I was in the private sector, I realized that money was the first component of any discussion about business and professional relationships, and I understood why. I was making enough in my other jobs that any additional monies would not have changed my lifestyle in any material way, but I don't work for nothing. Being paid is part of the job. The more people were willing to pay, the more they were committed to the idea, and the greater the likelihood that the association would be a positive one. So money was always important. Common sense dictates you should be paid for your work — whatever the market will bear.

"Fifty dollars a column," he said.

I'd thought this would be fun, but I said to him, "I wouldn't cross the street for fifty dollars."

"Well, then, what would it take?" he pressed. "How much to get you to write for us every week?"

I had no idea. "Two hundred and fifty dollars," I said. I took the figure out of the air. It seemed like a good number.

"We're a small paper," he responded.

"I understand," I said. "Call me back when you get bigger."

And he did. The very next day. The paper was part of a small chain of local newspapers, and Tom persuaded the parent company to run my reviews in all of its papers. So I became a movie reviewer. My friends thought I was nuts. They knew how much I loved going to the movies, and they knew how part of that enjoyment flowed from going out to dinner afterward to discuss the picture, but they still didn't get that this was something I could do. My sister Pat told me I was being ridiculous. "You have no idea how to write film criticism," she said, or words to that effect.

But that was precisely the point. I didn't see the job as having anything to do with film criticism. I was convinced there was a way to do it that would set me apart from other movie critics. After all, I wasn't a professional critic. I was a moviegoer, and I would approach my reviews with this distinction in mind. I would treat them like one of the post-movie discussions I always had with friends. I wouldn't review the lighting, or the cinematography. I'd write about whether I enjoyed the story, the whole movie. I'd tell readers if it made me laugh or cry or think, if it was believable. What people want to know, at bottom, is whether the reviewer liked the movie or not, so I would cut right to it. At the top of each review, I'd give the movie a plus or minus rating. I didn't believe in any of the usual one- to four-star nonsense. Either I'd like a movie enough to recommend it, or I wouldn't, and that would be it. My language would signal how much I liked or disliked a film.

It turned out to be one of the more enjoyable enterprises of my "third act" — and I'm still at it. The reviews are now syndicated in seven regional newspapers, including *Dan's Paper*, the unofficial voice of the Hamptons, which means that on rainy summer afternoons, the transplanted New York community on Long Island's East End must sometimes look to me for my picks and pans. I get a tremendous kick out of that. In all, according to the publisher, my reviews are read by more than 800,000 people each week, using the combined circulations of all seven newspapers. In fact, I've become so well known for the reviews that in 1999 I was hired as a critic by the Madison Square Garden cable network, so now I reach a much larger audience, in two media.

What's worth noting here is that this particular turn of events had almost nothing to do with the professional turns that preceded it. You have to be open to new ideas, to new opportunities, especially as you get on in years. I believe this deeply. Sometimes, it's the least likely prospect that sustains you and helps keep you young. For me, it happened to be reviewing movies, but it could be anything: running for local office, if that's where your interests lie, volunteering for a candidate, or going back to school to get a law degree or a business degree. Often, it's whatever takes you by surprise and pushes you in new directions. Or it's whatever you haven't done before and have been too afraid to try.

In my case, it wasn't just reviewing movies. Soon I was writing a weekly column for a major metropolitan daily. Peter Kalikow, then publisher of the *New York Post*, asked if I would consider writing for the Op-Ed page. Of course it was something I would consider; if you want to know the truth, I considered it plenty, but now that the opportunity was upon me there were some things to take into account. Here again, the custom was for columnists to deliver far more than I thought myself capable of delivering, and I told Peter I could write only one column a week. Typically, newspaper columnists write two or three times a week, but I figured I'd be lucky to come up with one good idea a week. Most people don't realize how difficult it is to write a political column, or a column of social commentary. The writing itself, if you're practiced at it, comes relatively easy; it's the ideas that come hard. You try to be timely, and you try not to repeat arguments you've seen or heard elsewhere, and more often than not you come up scratching your head, wondering how in the world you'll ever fill your allotted space. I have enormous respect for the men and women who somehow manage to fill their assigned spaces in inventive ways, because I know how difficult it is.

Soon, I enjoyed some success in this area as well. The people in charge of circulation at the *Post* informed me early on that they sold twelve thousand additional copies of the newspaper each Friday, the day my column appeared, than any other day of the week. I don't know for certain if there was any direct link between my column and the surge in readership (it's possible the bump was due to weekend movie listings), but the statistic was enormously gratifying, just as the work was enormously gratifying. What was especially satisfying was the way my columns often hit their mark. I'd always known the power of the press, but here I was able to see it from the other side of the table. As mayor, I could appreciate the enormous influence a local reporter could have on city politics, but now, as a local reporter myself, it was as if I were coming to this realization for the first time. It was a heady thing, at my advanced age, to have such an impact.

Perhaps the best example of this came as a result of a column I wrote in March 1992 on the hostile rhetoric flowing from the Bush administration concerning Israel. I wrote that when Secretary of State James Baker was castigated at a White House meeting for his belligerent stance toward Israel, he dismissed the charge with the comment "Fuck 'em. They [the Jews] didn't vote for us."

I was careful not to imply that Baker's remarks were anti-Semitic, although I was well aware they could be read as just that. Rather, I suggested they were merely crude and careless comments, tossed off by a man who disregarded Jewish leaders and voters in this one matter. The quote, when it appeared in print for the first time in my column, was extremely controversial, as I knew it would be, and I quietly relished all the attention, even though a good deal of it was negative and directed at me. It was a big international story (front page, in many cities), and my column was at the center of it. Fueling the controversy was the fact that I wouldn't reveal my source for the antagonistic quote.

Al Hunt, *The Wall Street Journal's* Washington bureau chief, was one of the quicker media watchdogs on the attack. "Eddie Koch is even less credible as a journalist than as a politician," he said on CNN, a comment that might have rankled if I were anything less than prepared to stand by my story. But I had it on good authority, from an unimpeachable source who was in the room at the time of Baker's comment, that the secretary of state had indeed uttered these words, and I would have put my credibility up against any other reporter's. Moreover, I was prepared to confront Baker directly, if I was given the opportunity.

As it turned out, I was given an even better opportunity. I received a letter from President Bush himself, written on the day my column appeared, in which he stated: "Ed, I never ever heard such ugliness out of Jim Baker." The president was critical of my decision to quote an unidentified source as the root of my story, and he pressed me on it. "I don't know who allegedly would report to have heard such a statement," he wrote, "but I simply do not believe the allegation." He signed the letter by hand, and added a personal note: "P.S. In spite of this 'flap' your #1 fan remains BPB [meaning the First Lady] — she sends her best."

Talk about remaining relevant! There I

was, over two years out of office, a commentator by profession, and the president of the United States was taking time out of his busy schedule to respond to one of my columns. I don't think I ever enjoyed such a direct, public link to such high office, either as a congressman or as mayor. And even if I had, I never enjoyed it more. There followed a series of exchanges with the president on the subject of Israel, and upon each I reflected on what a rare and good thing it was for a private citizen — a journalist, even — to have the president's ear on a subject of such vital importance. Believe me, I bent that ear to full advantage — and, I think, with positive results. "I believe the special relationship between the U.S. and Israel," I wrote in one of my follow-up letters, "which began with Harry Truman and continued with Ronald Reagan, has been considerably weakened. I hope I'm wrong."

As an American Jew, remembering how the world declined to help the Jews when they were under assault and being murdered by the Nazis, I am always concerned with the security of Israel, and the protection of Jewish communities under attack somewhere in the world, every day of the year. I have attempted to use my various platforms — as mayor, as columnist, and as commentator — to influence U.S. foreign policy in this area at least indirectly. However, regular readers of my column, which is now carried every Friday in the *Daily News*, know that my issues are "catholic" — that is, they're universal, and not limited to this very important cause.

My stint at the *Post* was interrupted by a change in management. Abe Hirschfeld took over, and I quit when he fired my friend Eric Brindel, the editorial page editor. I immediately accepted an offer from another friend, Mort Zuckerman, to take my column to the rival *Daily News*. However, about a week or so later I got a call at home on a Sunday from Rupert Murdoch, who had just bought the *Post* in bankruptcy court and hoped to turn things around. He asked me to come back.

"Rupert," I said, "I'm so upset with myself. It's painful because I owe you a lot, but I can't. I made an agreement with the *News*." My "debt" to Murdoch was his newspaper's front-page endorsement of me during my 1977 Democratic primary run for mayor — making the *Post* the first metropolitan newspaper to come out for my candidacy, providing an enormous lift to my campaign, and helping me to a primary runoff victory over Mario Cuomo.

Murdoch's endorsement was on the merits, I believed then and now, and he never asked for anything in return, but I never forgot it. And yet here I was, turning him down in his first request of me over the many years since he helped me to win the office.

"Do you have a contract?" Rupert asked.

"No," I replied, "but I've shaken hands with Mort and I can't go back on that any more than you would."

He understood, but he wasn't giving up just yet. "How long is your deal?" he asked.

"Nothing's final," I said, "but we discussed a year."

"Would you come back after that?"

"Yes," I said. "I would." And I did. After what Rupert Murdoch did for me, I owed it to him.

Incidentally, those 1977 primary results were extraordinarily close: I got 21 percent of the vote to Cuomo's 20 percent. Abe Beame, the incumbent, tallied 19 percent. In a field that also included Bella Abzug and Herman Badillo, the top six candidates were separated by fewer than eighty thousand votes, so clearly the *Post*'s endorsement was one of the key determining factors, and I was only too happy to return to the fold.

I later left the *Post* a second time, for reasons having nothing to do with Rupert

Murdoch, and landed once again at the *News*, where I remain as of this writing. I left the *Post* because I felt uncomfortable with its new editor, John Podhoretz, and his very conservative policies, and Mort Zuckerman generously welcomed me back to the *News*. With all the back-and-forth between the city's two main tabloids, I don't think I've missed more than a week or two between contracts. My column has been a fixture on the New York scene for nearly a decade, and I am immensely proud of the body of work I've built up over the years — fifty-two columns a year. What I've learned, in the doing, is that there is no set way to write a weekly column. The approach I've come up with works well for me. First, I struggle with an idea. In this, I am not alone. Columnists are always hoping for an original idea, or an unusual approach to an issue. That's the hardest part, coming up with a concept that doesn't seem tired, but once I land on an idea I immediately put my thoughts down on paper. I write my first draft on a Friday, and this is all-important. That first draft can be terrible, but I have concluded that you can't write a strong column on a single pass. At least I can't. I need to put something down on paper, and work from there, and by the end of the day I have a draft that is at least a starting point. Then I take it home and work on it over the weekend. On Monday, I send it around to six trusted friends and associates (two of them are my law partners, Jim Gill and Austin Campriello). They read it, and offer their comments. Some of their suggestions I take, and some I don't, but I find the collective input tremendously useful.

Finally, by the end of the day on Wednesday, I submit the piece, and from the comments I've collected over the years from my editors at the *News* and the *Post*, very few columns are in such good form when they are handed in, both in syntax and ideas. At the *Post*, they hardly ever touched a word, although at the *News*, they find wonderful ways to tighten the language to make the column even stronger. I've yet to meet a writer who cannot benefit from a strong editor.

I could, I suppose, write a column in a more timely fashion, on deadline, but for the most part I choose not to. I like the approach I've developed. Occasionally, on a breaking story that demands immediate attention, I might at the request of my editor scrap a more thoughtful, thoroughgoing piece I've been working on for one tied to the news, and in those instances the columns are never as thoughtful. They might be timely, and there might be no avoiding them, but I always wish I could rework them another day or two before sending them out for public consumption. But such are the demands of the newspaper business that you can't always take all the time you need; sometimes you must make do with all the time you have.

I'm told my columns have gotten stronger the longer I've been doing them, and I am not inclined to argue. On the eve of the U.S. Senate impeachment vote, I compared the passing of Jordan's King Hussein to the dead legacy of President Bill Clinton. "Two world leaders were laid to rest this week," I wrote. "One physically, the other metaphysically." I thought that was a pretty strong lead, and I went on to reflect on how history would remember each world leader. "It is rumored the President has prattled that he believes he won this battle," I concluded. "He is in error. From now on, every schoolchild should and will be taught that the life of Bill Clinton establishes that those in public office who forswear integrity and decency are doomed first to ridicule, then to oblivion."

Quite effective. I think.

In another, I championed the potential

candidacy of Hillary Clinton, who in February 1999 was publicly contemplating a run for the U.S. Senate from New York. Her likely opponent, it was felt, would be Rudolph Giuliani, whom I helped become mayor of New York but now oppose. "I hope she'll run, but it won't be a cakewalk," I wrote. "She would be up against a ruthless adversary who is willing to play the demagogue if it helps his cause." In my mind, I couldn't be too harsh on Giuliani. "If there is a low road available," I wrote, "trust him to walk it."

"It takes a state to elect a senator," I offered, in signing off that column, and after it appeared it was pointed out to me by some Giuliani critics that because of my uniquely positive relationship with New York Democrats, and my uniquely adversarial relationship with Giuliani, I would perhaps be one of the few individuals whose endorsement might turn such a contest in Mrs. Clinton's favor. I welcomed the opportunity then, and as this book goes to press I still look forward to it, because there is nothing like deploying your relevance and influence to ensure that the right things happen to the right people, for the right reasons.

Several weeks later, Hillary Clinton called to thank me for my comments on her entering the race. I told her she should make health care and national comprehensive health insurance her major issue. I also said she should publicly apologize for her ineffectiveness when she first took on the issue, early in President Clinton's first term, while at the same time acknowledging that the issue is still with us, and that forty-three million Americans are without medical insurance. She agreed with me on virtually every point, and subsequently discussed these matters publicly along the suggested lines.

And so you see I have my hand (and my head and heart) in all manner of things. Since leaving City Hall, I've worked in radio, television, newspapers, advertising . . . you name it. I also lecture quite frequently. When I first left office, I did fifty-five paid speeches a year, for three straight years. These days, I keep the annual total to around twenty or twenty-five. One of the few concessions I've made to what others have traditionally termed "old age" is to cut back on my business travel. I don't care how old you are, it wears on you after a while, hopping in and out of planes, staying overnight in a strange city. I'm happy to do it from time to time, for an important appearance, and I do on occasion fly to California or Florida to give a speech, but there are plenty of lecture opportunities within an hour's car ride from New York City, which is close enough to get me back to my apartment after my evening appearances.

I've also taught for some years now at New York University, and beginning in January 1999 at Brandeis University in Waltham, Massachusetts, just outside Boston, where I signed on for one semester as the Fred and Rita Richman Distinguished Visiting Professor of Politics to teach a class called "A Political Experience." The logistics of this were interesting. I shared teaching duties with a visiting professor named Garrison Nelson, from the University of Vermont. I flew into Boston every Monday morning to lecture on planned topics concerning the governance of New York City, such as Transportation, Public Relations, Economic Revitalization, Ethnic Affairs, and Gay Rights. I asked thirteen friends who had served in my administration to join me, one at each of my thirteen weekly lectures, to discuss their experiences with that day's topic. Before class, I would sit for office hours, although regrettably few students came, even though the class, with 150 students enrolled, was always well attended. After class, I would fly home. It was a full day, but entirely manageable. Admittedly, my lecture style was not what it could have been at first. I tended to confront students for thoughtless answers to some of my questions, in much the same way I challenged some of the callers to my radio show. Some students complained about my style, but others defended me in the student newspaper. Throughout my career, friends and critics have complained about that style, and I respond to both groups in the same way. I tell them I didn't get where I am on the strength of my personality, and I have no intention of changing. I don't think it's possible to change this late in the game. It's a part of who I am — a Sagittarius, born on December 12, and candor is our principal characteristic.

The class met for a second day each week with a lecture by Professor Nelson, who assigned papers and gave tests and offered final grades. I must say, of all the hats I've worn since being mayor, I think I got the biggest kick out of being a professor, and I'm gratified that I wasn't put off by the long-distance arrangement because as it turned out it was hardly an inconvenience. And it was thoroughly enjoyable!

In all, I currently have nine jobs. I've had more, and one day, no doubt, I'll have fewer.

But I believe the turns in my professional life reveal an important point: Your career is what *you* make of *it*, not what *it* makes of *you*. If you mean to take something home from your job other than a paycheck, and if you mean to keep taking that something home long after the traditional age of retirement, then you need to keep an open mind on what is available to you. I understand that most of you reading this book are not former New York City mayors and therefore will not have the same kinds of opportunities available to you as I've had. However, the point I want to drive home is that there *are* opportunities. Wherever you live, whatever you've done with your so-called peak career years, however you choose to fill the days of what you may or may not think of as your retirement . . . there are fulfilling experiences just waiting to be had. In my own life, the best illustration of this took me completely by surprise. It had nothing to do with almost everything that preceded it — and yet at the same time it was almost a too-perfect coalescing of the many skills I had picked up over the years. It didn't last forever, but then what good job ever does? While it lasted, it was an eye-opening, challenging, and lucrative experience — and it changed my public profile in ways I could never have imagined. Who would have thought, at my age, that I would become the star of a daytime television series? I'm as good-looking as the next guy, but when you take me from the realm of public affairs, I'm out of my element. When I sat down with my good friend Allen Schwartz to explore my career opportunities, I never even considered becoming a judge on a syndicated courtroom show.

But you never know . . . right?

four

The People's Court

Have you ever noticed how sometimes it is the least likely path that takes you where you're most delighted to be? Think back over the crossroad moments in your life, and you will undoubtedly be surprised at how your prospects once looked compared with how they now stand. Moreover, you'll find that an initial career somehow paved the way for a succeeding career, without planning or forethought, or that one opportunity inevitably led to another. At least, it's been that way with me, going back to childhood and running all the way through my three terms as mayor. It's even followed me from public life into the private sector.

The older I get, the more I believe in things like serendipity and fate — and the next twist to life after City Hall had large helpings of each. In 1997, the least likely of paths was laid out for me by my agent (and friend), Jim Griffin of the William Morris Agency, whose marching orders were to steer me in new directions. I told him that if something sounded good to him it would probably sound good to me, and yet he called me up one morning with a job opportunity so far off the map I wouldn't have even bothered to chart it. Would I be interested, he wanted to know, in presiding over a revamped version of one of the most successful syndicated daytime television programs? Specifically, would I consider filling the seat on the "bench" vacated by Judge Joseph Wapner, the retired California judge who hosted the popular program *The People's Court* for a number of years, disposing of small claims cases before a national television audience?

I thought, Me, a judge? I rather liked the idea, even if it only meant playing a judge on television. (Remember those old commercials? "I'm not a doctor but I play one on TV.") I especially liked it for the serendipitous way it seemed to reinforce what I had long thought would be one of my major legacies as mayor: the desperately needed reform of the city's judicial system. It may not have reinforced this for anyone but me, but I took my validation wherever I could find it, especially on matters of such lasting importance. See, one of my priorities, after I was inaugurated as mayor, was to formulate a merit-based selection process to fill the courtroom vacancies that would inevitably occur during my administration, throughout the city. That such a nonpolitical selection process took hold on my watch, and that I was now being asked to assume the role of a judge on television myself, I chalked up to fate. Like I said, I'm a firm believer in such things, and here fate was staring me full in the face.

Let me first set up the present-day, Hollywood aspects of this story, before doubling back to explain my attempts at judicial reform; in my thinking, the two go hand in hand. Like many people, I was aware of *The People's Court* during its first run. As mayor, I happened to be fairly busy during the day, when the show was on, so I rarely watched it, but I was aware of the format and its popularity. I knew its place on the cultural landscape. When a parody turned up, on *Saturday Night Live*, or in some other context, I understood the joke. As a matter of fact, I was surprised to learn the show had gone off the air and had been in reruns, because within the previous year I had been asked by a local cable program to comment (for entertainment purposes) on several of Judge Wapner's decisions. I might have been even more surprised to learn that the producers were considering reviving it, but I knew enough about the entertainment industry to recognize that nothing succeeds in theory like an old idea. Whether it succeeds *in fact* is often another matter, but at least if you have a track record and a built-in familiarity with audiences you've got a shot.

It was an interesting offer, but when Jim first laid it out for me it didn't feel entirely right. Primarily, I was concerned about the scheduling; with everything I had going on, I didn't see how I could slot in a production schedule for a daily show, and I wasn't sure it made sense even to try. Also, I wasn't sure I saw myself as a television judge (really, an arbitrator), whose job it was primarily to entertain; I wasn't sure it was the image I wanted to project to the rest of the country. Everything I'd been doing since the mayoralty had been geared toward advancing my own ideas and my own persona, and here I was essentially being asked to be judiciously circumspect, while at the same time presiding over an entertainment program, as opposed to offering candid, off-the-cuff commentary on a news program.

"You know, Jim," I said, "I've got all this other stuff going on, and this television court show is on every day."

"It doesn't work that way, Ed," he explained. "You could probably do a week's worth of shows in two days, afternoons and evenings. They could work around your schedule."

This was good to know.

"And you know," he continued, "shows like this are big bucks, about a million dollars a year."

One million dollars? For a couple days' work each week? I thought back to my salary as mayor — $60,000 to start, $130,000 by the time the people threw me out — and I wondered at the disparity. Obviously, being mayor of New York City was a far more important, far more demanding job than presiding over a television courtroom, but public service rarely pays well when compared with salaries in the private sector. Those who choose public service don't usually do it for the money; they tend to be dedicated individuals who want to leave a positive mark on society and in the history books, and to improve the lives of others. Besides, I'd tried never to make a professional decision based on money, because in truth I had all I needed. Money is not all that important to me, so long as I have enough of it to buy what I want and live the way I want to live. That sounds trite, I know, but I have modest needs. I live alone, in a two-bedroom apartment with a terrace. I love my apartment, and I wouldn't even think about moving. I hope to live there until my time is done.

I am a creature of habit, and in my case those habits were all developed on a public servant's salary. I like nice clothes, but I rarely buy anything unless it's on sale at Brooks Brothers. I think I have one of everything they sell in the men's department, most of which I've gotten over the years on sale. I never wear anything out, and I never throw anything away. I am certainly not extravagant. I lease a car, but I don't have a vacation home. When I vacation, which is not often, I am usually invited as a guest to a friend's summer home, or to my sister's cottage in Amagansett, on Long Island's East End. It's not that I'm too cheap to spring for a hotel room, but it doesn't occur to me to leave home unless I am invited by people with whom I enjoy spending time — and they wouldn't have it any other way. I don't even go to Broadway shows all that often, because of the price of theater tickets, which now runs between $75 and $100 for orchestra seats. Shows are too often disappointing, especially when compared with the new movies that open every week. I can afford to waste $75, taking a chance on a show, but I don't like the long odds against seeing a good one. If I go to a terrible movie, on the other hand, and it costs $8 or $9, I don't feel like I've been taken to the cleaners. But at $75 a ticket, a show's got to create a special memory if I'm to feel it was worth it. Unfortunately, those special memories are rare.

"Are you interested?" Jim pressed.

"Sure I'm interested," I said, with only the one moment of hesitation I needed to consider the aspects of the proposal. "I'm interested in new challenges."

Jim told me to expect a call from Stu Billett, the producer of the show, who lived in California. Stu called the very next day and told me he was coming into town and would like to meet with me, so I invited him to lunch at the Four Seasons, which is one of my favorite restaurants, and a terrific setting for a business lunch. The room is the most beautiful in the city, the staff is supremely attentive, and the tables are far enough apart that you can speak freely with your dining companions without worrying that the people at the adjacent tables are listening in. Stu mentioned that he'd never been to the Four Seasons, so I knew it would be a treat for him. I don't dine there often enough to have my own table waiting for me, as Henry Kissinger, Lew and Jack Rudin, and Mort Zuckerman do, but I am known there and I am also treated like one of the regulars. (The regulars know to eat lunch in the Grill Room and never in the dining room, with the extraordinary pool — that's for dinner.)

I realize that my choice of restaurant puts me somewhat at odds with my previous statement that I am a man of modest tastes, so let me explain. I *am* a man of modest tastes, but those tastes occasionally include expensive restaurants. It is, I guess, one of my few indulgences. I do have a car and driver, who happens to be a retired police officer and is relied upon more for security and peace of mind than he is for his driving. I pay for these "luxuries," but I regard them as necessities. When you've been in the public eye as long as I have, you tend to attract your share of kooks and wackos, and I don't consider my precaution to be a luxury in any sense.

Stu and I hit it off right away. I liked him enormously, and he seemed to like me. I liked his ideas for the show, and how he saw the judge's role. The way he walked me through it, I realized my credibility wouldn't be an issue. There'd be no pandering to the audience, no stunts, no embarrassing television theatrics to trump up ratings. The format, as before, was to be a straightforward courtroom setting, with interesting litigants arguing what Stu hoped would be compelling civil disputes.

In its initial ten-year run, *The People's Court* was produced in California, but Stu wanted to move production to New York, to bring a different feel to the kinds of cases that would be available to him — and, correspondingly, to the kinds of litigants that would be available. In so doing, he wanted to cast a judge who represented New York, and he told me he'd always thought of me as the quintessential New Yorker. I was flattered. It wasn't the first time I'd heard the phrase applied to me, although to be frank I never truly understood why. I lead a relatively quiet life. I don't run around with fast-track friends. I don't go to many parties or chic gatherings. And yet I am thought of by many as the quintessential New Yorker. Apparently, as mayor, I somehow managed to impose my personality on the city, to where the one was closely identified with the other, and, believe me, I am certainly delighted and proud of the connection. It's better than being called the quintessential American — that title is for a midwesterner — or the quintessential former politician, soon to be forgotten.

At the end of the lunch, which had gone rather well, I reached for the check without thinking about it. The difference between me reaching for the check and some others I know reaching for the check is that I mean to pay it. Stu meant to pay for it, too. He said, "No, no, I'll pay for it. I suggested the meeting."

"That's true," I allowed, my hand still on the bill, "but I invited you to lunch. This is my city, and I chose the restaurant."

He said, "Okay."

A lot of times, you'll have an awkward back-and-forth before someone finally bows out, but here Stu could see that I had every intention of treating him to lunch. He said, "This may be the first time in the history of television that the talent has picked up the check."

I laughed — and inwardly I glowed at the term "talent." There it was again. I tried to think of a parallel example, wherein we define ourselves by our abilities, not by what we do but how we do it, and I came up empty. I also liked that he referred to me as the talent, because he hadn't yet offered me the job. I might have had talent, I might have even *been* the talent, but I wasn't *his* talent just yet. We had danced around a direct job offer during the lunch, and we talked about what the show might look like with me on the bench, but it was meant to be an introduction, an exploratory meeting. We never discussed any kind of business deal. That is, we never discussed any kind of deal until I paid for lunch, because as soon as I signed the credit card slip he offered me the job. No screen test. No committee of colleagues he had to discuss it with back in Los Angeles. No trial of any kind.

"You want the job?" he asked.

"Sure," I said. And that was that. He didn't offer it to me *just* because I'd turned the tables and picked up the check, but it set a mood. Frankly, I knew it would have an impact, but that's not why I did it. I did it because it was the right thing to do, the polite thing to do. If I'd been in Los Angeles, and we were eating at a restaurant of Stu's choice, I would have certainly allowed him to pay for it, but here in New York, in my city, under these circumstances, he was my guest. After I joined the show, Stu and I had many dinners together, but he never again let me pick up the check, and I didn't argue.

Now, I had some fairly strong ideas about judges and how they should conduct themselves — in a real courtroom setting, or in a television studio, as an arbitrator. This is where the notion of fate came in. I've been critical of our judicial system and individual judges since 1963, when I became a Democratic district leader on the New York County Democratic Executive Committee, also known as Tammany Hall, after I defeated Carmine DeSapio for the position in a party election. DeSapio, who once held the title of county leader — or, colloquially, the Boss of Bosses — is now in his eighties, frail, and living on Fifth Avenue, a block away from my apartment in Greenwich Village, but back then he held enormous influence over our city and our courts. Under DeSapio, almost all judges, whether elected or appointed, owed their positions to him. Even after DeSapio's defeat, mayors still used judgeships for political appointments. I changed all that.

Like every mayor before me facing a vacancy in the criminal or family courts, I had absolute power to appoint as judge any lawyer I chose, provided the appointee was a resident of New York City and had been a lawyer for at least ten years. Every mayor before me, going back to John Lindsay, appointed some people to the bench who were professionally unqualified. In December 1977, one month before he left office, Abe Beame appointed ten people as judges who were found by the City Bar Association to be unqualified.

I created by executive order a new merit-based system of judicial appointments, which provided for a twenty-seven-member mayoral judiciary committee. I appointed the chair, and twelve of its members; the two presiding justices of the First and Second Departments of the Appellate Division of the State Supreme Court, which includes New York City, each appointed another six members; and, on a rotating basis, the deans of various law schools in the city would be called on to appoint the other two members. Under this formula, fewer than half of the committee members would be appointed by the mayor. The committee, not the mayor, would seek out the candidates and propose three for each criminal- and family-court vacancy to me. I would interview all three and select one for appointment to the court.

The mayor's appointments didn't have to be confirmed by the New York City Council. When the governor appointed a judge, the appointment had to be confirmed by the New York State Senate. When the president appointed a judge, the appointment had to be confirmed by the U.S. Senate.

One of the very first public events I attended after the 1977 election was a gathering of ABNY — the Association for a Better New York, a great civic organization and booster of the city, formed by Lew Rudin, who remains its chairman, its heart, and its soul. There in the audience were former mayors John Lindsay and Robert Wagner, Abe Beame's immediate predecessors. Unlike previous mayors, I said in my ABNY address, I was going to make judicial selection totally devoid of politics. I looked out at the crowd, and I could hear Lindsay and Wagner, who were sitting close to the stage and whispering to each other, saying, "Isn't that what we did?" And I said to myself, No, that's not what you did. What you did was also a progressive step but not as far-reaching as what I was doing. You selected candidates yourselves and then submitted them to your mayor's Judiciary Committee and the City Bar Association Committee, which then determined if the candidates were "professionally qualified." Well, that didn't seem to me the standard we should be using if we were looking for the best available candidates. There's a big gap between being professionally qualified and being the best available candidate. But even then my predecessors violated their own minimum standards by appointing people who had been rejected by one or both of these advisory committees.

My commitment to excellence and impartiality extended to interim appointments of civil court judges, provided in the law when vacancies occurred before the next election. Most important, I pledged that at the end of each judge's ten-year term, he or she would be evaluated by the Mayor's Judiciary Committee and the City Bar Association Committee. If the committees jointly recommended reappointment, I would reappoint the judge, without exception. If either of the committees recommended against reappointment, I would not reappoint that person, without exception.

The reforms were put to the test almost right away. A judge who had been appointed by a prior administration came up for review at the end of his ten-year term. He had been a consumer affairs commissioner for the mayor who put him on the bench, and as far as I knew he was an accomplished, highly regarded judge. However, one of the committees recommended against reappointment, and because of my commitment I was bound by their conclusion. What happened was predictable in that this candidate had a lot of friends in high places, and I got a number of calls on his behalf. One judge on the Appellate Division First Department called to tell me what a mistake I was making in not reappointing this sitting judge, and urged me to overrule my committee.

"Judge," I said, "you're wasting your time. I made my commitment on this issue. Whatever the committee decides on reappointment, right or wrong, is binding on me."

Efforts were made by some to get the committee to reverse itself, but the committee didn't change its position, and I didn't reappoint this patrician judge. The interesting aftermath was that he was later made a federal magistrate. He was good enough, by whatever standards were in place, to sit on the federal bench, but not good enough to sit on New York City's criminal or family courts.

In the course of my administration, there were perhaps eight or ten candidates who, for various reasons, were not reappointed at the end of their terms. Of the ten last-minute appointments I inherited from the Beame administration, for example, roughly half were recommended for reappointment by the two judiciary committees at the end of their initial ten-year term, and half were not. And the ones who were recommended were given a second term by me, despite the circumstances of their original appointment. Like it or not, I followed the protocol, without exception.

I believe my judicial reforms were among the greatest contributions of my administration, and I left office confident they would stand for generations, if not forever. David Dinkins, my immediate successor, to his credit extended my executive order and continued the selection process in essentially the same manner as I had done for the previous twelve years. Four years later, Rudolph Giuliani initially extended the executive order, then in his second year in office he quietly changed the process. More accurately, he gutted it. His counsel, Denny Young, called and told me they were thinking of reducing the size of the Mayor's Judicial Committee, from twenty-seven to nineteen, and he asked my opinion of the proposed change. I advised against it, saying that if it ain't broke, as the aphorism goes, don't fix it. However, Giuliani did more than reduce the size of the committee: He stripped it of its major power, and its purpose. On July 20, 1994, he declared he would no longer be bound by its decisions on reappointments. By the new protocol, the mayor could reappoint judges who were rejected and reject judges who were recommended for reappointment, and he did both.

I was furious, and I criticized the mayor's action, publicly and often. While I was no longer in an elected position of authority, I had some public influence. I had my radio show, my newspaper column, my television commentaries, and my teaching appointment at New York University. I had the ears of many opinion-makers and decision-makers, and I was prepared to bend them, big time. I used every means available to denounce Giuliani on this matter. (I denounced him on other matters as well, as his administration dragged on, but this was always the major issue and the major source of my disenchantment with him.) Under Giuliani's selection system, judges seeking reappointment no longer had to worry about convincing committees of their peers of their fitness for the job, or reappointment. They had to convince only the mayor that they should be reappointed, a situation that vested Giuliani with enormous power to terrorize these judges, threatening their independence for the balance of their careers on the bench. Understand, in accepting their appointments in the first place, most judges end their professional opportunities as heavy-duty lawyers. It's difficult if not impossible to return to the private sector. They have spouses, children, obligations. Their salaries exceed $100,000 but are nowhere near what a first-rate lawyer makes in private practice. Today, an able first-year lawyer in a first-rate law firm commands an annual salary of over $100,000. I thought it was awful that Giuliani had changed the judicial selection process so that some judges who were not of sufficient courage might lose their independence.

Is "terror" too harsh a word to use in this context? I don't believe so. It takes an incredibly courageous man or woman to make some of the decisions our judges are called on to make, and if that courage is threatened by external factors, such as the continued ability to earn an adequate living and support a family, then we all should worry. Our public interests would no longer be served. The City of New York is itself the largest litigant in commercial matters in our city courts, and many of the criminal and family court judges serve as acting Supreme Court judges, trying very important cases. And in the criminal courts, the city (known as "The People") is effectively a party in every case.

I spoke out against the mayor on this issue at every opportunity. I published an article in the *New York City Law Review*, edited by the students of The City University of New York School of Law, outlining some of the terrible results of the mayor's vitiation of the selection process. Let me tell you, he was not happy about all the *Sturm und Drang* I was making. At one point, stung by the criticism, he called a press conference and denounced my prior judicial appointments. He called me hypocritical and conveyed that I had appointed political hacks. I said to myself, This man doesn't tell the truth. If you criticize him, he seeks to destroy you and unfairly attacks your integrity. He doesn't simply defend himself or justify his own actions; he looks, instead, to discredit and demonize his adversaries. He claimed at the press conference to have investigated my judicial appointments when he was U.S. Attorney, which he never had. If he had investigated me, he surely would have interviewed judges, talked to people in my administration, and perhaps even subpoenaed me. He would have issued a public report. He would have done *something*. But he didn't do anything. He didn't care about that. His stock-in-trade was innuendo, and then he went further, holding up a copy of the Jack Newfield book *City for Sale*, which focused on allegations of corruption during my third term. He said, "It's all in here."

It was an appalling display. And nobody questioned it. That's the way Giuliani operates. With respect to any corruption by anyone in my administration, I took full political responsibility for what occurred on my watch, but no one ever charged or believed that I was personally corrupt. The Newfield book said that I was personally honest, and there was nothing in the book about my judicial appointments to the criminal and family courts, but Giuliani held it up like a prop, as some kind of validation that I had done something wrong in the appointment of judges. The only reporter at the press conference who even bothered to read the book, to see if there was any derogative commentary on my judicial selection process and the merit system, was Joyce Purnick of *The New York Times*, who has since been named the paper's Metro Section editor; she wrote that there was, in fact, nothing at all in the book about my judicial appointments. Giuliani's viciousness was never more evident.

Ruining reputations is Giuliani's passion, but my reputation was too good for him to ruin. Most people don't operate from the same position of strength as I do, having more than one bully pulpit from which to reply, and as I moved about town during the ensuing debate on judicial appointments I kept hearing from many people in the legal community who were afraid to speak up on the matter. Privately, lawyers would tell me how important it was for me to challenge the mayor on this issue, but they wouldn't criticize Giuliani out of fear that their clients doing business with the city would somehow receive unfavorable treatment as a result. One Friday evening during this time, I participated in a B'nai Jeshurun Synagogue service, at my sister's request, and ran into one of the most acclaimed lawyers in the city, who said to me, "Ed, keep it up." He was referring to my criticism of Giuliani, and I said to myself, You prick! Why aren't *you* speaking up? You're one of the premier lawyers in this town. If you think my voice is louder than yours, you're crazy. But I held my tongue. I had terrible thoughts about this man, and about all the others just like him who remained silent on the issue, but I said nothing.

I'm sorry to report that the City Bar Association, in order to have some role in the selection process, consented to the mayor's statement that he now reserved the power to overrule its veto on reappointment decisions. Still, I was fiercely proud of my efforts to preserve the integrity of the judicial selection process. People who are involved with cleaning up the judiciary know what we achieved, and I mention those achievements here not to take a bow but to establish that I'd spent a good deal of time thinking through what makes a good judge. Independence is key — whether you're serving in family or criminal court or on a television soundstage trying cases under an arbitration agreement. A good judge is primarily a good listener. He must know what questions to ask, what areas to pursue. He must be fair in fact and in appearance. I have always been aware of the statement in the Old Testament, and in the Ethics of the Fathers, that thunders: "Justice, justice, shalt thou render saith the Lord."

For all of the reasons I've detailed here, I took the prospect of presiding in a courtroom fairly seriously, even if the courtroom was to be a television set in a Manhattan studio. Our cases were to be pulled from real courtrooms around the country, with the overwhelming number coming from New

York City and the surrounding region (New Jersey, New York, Connecticut, and Pennsylvania), simply because of proximity. Our producers looked for compelling issues, interesting personalities, and unusual situations, and I must say I was surprised to learn that there were plenty of cases that fit one or more aspects of this description.

I served on *The People's Court* for two seasons, during which time we didn't stray much from our initial blueprint. We tried to keep it as much like a real courtroom as possible. I didn't meet our litigants before the taping. I learned the facts of the case as they were presented in court, as the parties and witnesses testified, except for reading the complaints shortly before each trial began. Just about the only significant difference between our courtroom and a real courtroom was the amount of time allotted to each case. On television the average case took about a half hour to try, and then it was edited down to about ten minutes for broadcast.

I had some trouble, for a while, with the balance between the judicial and the entertainment components of the program. In the beginning, I conducted myself in the manner I thought totally appropriate for a sitting judge. I asked questions, but mostly I listened. I was careful not to be a dominant personality. Well, here is where good television clashed with good courtroom presence, because Stu Billett came to my law office one morning early on in my run and said, "Ed, we want more of you, and your personality." I thought, This is television and Stu is absolutely right. The program was intended to be entertaining and educational, and I tried to marry the educational components of what we were doing with the law, all the while mindful of the entertainment value we were hoping to achieve. And so I interjected more than I had at the outset.

Compared with the other television judges and particularly with Judge Judy, who presided over the most popular syndicated courtroom program, I was relatively laid back. Judge Judy, whom I appointed to a real bench in New York City before her television career, has an extraordinary style. She lectures everybody. "I'm not stupid," she often tells the litigants, that being her trademark line. "Does it say 'Stupid' on my forehead?" The reasons for her success were an endless topic of conversation between Stu Billett and myself. Her audience was nine million nationwide, and mine was about three million. My producers naturally hoped and wanted *The People's Court* to be the number-one program, and hoped I would vie with Judge Judy in temperament, or that my laid-back, more judicial approach would somehow catch on. Neither came to pass.

When we first launched our respective programs, Judy and I were interviewed together on a program called *The Open Mind*, and she remarked that her style was different from mine, that she doesn't always apply the law to her cases and instead applies common sense. I thought, That's ridiculous! A real judge must apply the law, whether or not he or she agrees with it; the legislature has the right to change the law, not judges. Stu Billett suggested that Judy's show was popular for much the same reason that television wrestling or Jerry Springer was. No one admits to watching those kinds of programs, and yet they're the most popular shows going; pro wrestling has been on the air forever, despite the fact that everyone knows it's a charade.

To compensate for my more reserved demeanor, I tried to provide enough natural humor and energy to cover the lack of bloodletting. I could not bring myself to call people liars in order to raise the decibel level of our show, except of course when the lying was blatant and germane to my decision.

And yet despite the added focus on my personality, our ratings never soared and hardly even increased. They held steady, respectably so, but we pulled nowhere near the kind of numbers we needed in order to do well in a highly competitive marketplace.

During my second and final season, there were at least five different courtroom shows in syndication. For those of you who never saw my program, it went like this. We did three trials in an hour-long program, allowing for background and commentary and commercials. There was a law secretary on staff — Harvey Levin, who was also the show's coproducer, with Stu Billett — and a law clerk, and both were constantly busy researching relevant rulings while the case was heard. It was a tremendous time-saver.

For some reason, we got a lot of dog-bite cases, and as a result became involved in trying to change the law. New York has the most lenient dog-bite law on the books. In effect, the law gives every dog one free bite, because in order to hold the dog's owner responsible, you have to show that he or she had prior knowledge of the dog's vicious propensities and didn't take appropriate measures to control it. Think about it: You're walking in an unfamiliar neighborhood, and a dog bites you; it will often be impossible for you to establish prior knowledge of the animal's vicious propensities. In some states, it's far easier to hold the dog's owner accountable. In Connecticut, for example, where we got a lot of our cases, they have a much stronger law imposing strict liability, and we worked to change the law in New York to bring it more into line with our neighboring states. There was, alas, little interest in the legislature, and New Yorkers continue to be at a disadvantage in this regard. But it was important to make the attempt. Recently, in a case involving a horse that kicked and caused injury, the Appellate Division permitted a recovery based on negligence, suggesting a shift in such cases. It may be that in dog cases you can now prove liability on the theory of negligence. Time will tell, when a case is appealed to the Court of Appeals.

Our cases came from actual claims filed in small-claims courts awaiting trial. Our producers had staff monitoring local courts, and elsewhere, looking for litigants who agreed to be bound by my decision, waiving their right of appeal in order to appear on our program. In this respect, I wielded more direct influence than a judge in a bona fide courtroom because our litigants waived their right of appeal as a matter of contract.

Losers and winners alike received an appearance fee, and where a judgment was directed by me it was paid by the show, so it was a no-lose proposition for our litigants. I suppose, too, there was a certain element of Andy Warhol's fifteen minutes of fame at play in their decision to appear on our program. But people are people, and they argued their cases as vociferously as if they were personally on the line for the disputed amount. They were in need of being proven right, in front of an audience of their peers, and the desire to win — no matter what — showed itself every time.

In other respects, though, I had considerably less influence on the proceedings than a true courtroom judge, who holds the power of contempt. Oftentimes, the heated back-and-forth between litigants got rancorous, and it became difficult to control the mood of the courtroom because I did not have the power to hold people in contempt of court. I couldn't say, "If you keep that up, I'll fine you, or send you to jail." I couldn't dock their appearance fees, or any pending judgment in their favor. In truth, some of the litigants' misbehavior resulted in good television, although I tried to maintain control and for the most part was successful in doing so.

Sometimes I wondered, in a particular case, Is this *Tobacco Road,* or is this New York City? Really, you wouldn't believe some of the peculiar people who came into our courtroom. People sue each other over all kinds of things, some serious and legitimate and others less so: dog bites, custody of lost or stolen items, disputes over services rendered. We had one case involving six bridge chairs, and whether or not they were given as gifts or borrowed and not returned. The chairs, quite old, were worth a total of about $24, and we were taking extensive testimony.

Imagine a silly misunderstanding and chances are some version of it was arbitrated on our show, but we also heard valuable rights cases. In one, I ruled on the rightful ownership of a baseball that was hit into the stands by Mark McGwire for a double during the 1998 season, and was said to be worth thousands of dollars. The maximum I could award in New York's Small Claims Court was $3,000, but here I found for the defendant, who was in custody of the ball; after appearing on our program, he consigned the disputed ball to an auction house and sold it for an amount in excess of $20,000.

Perhaps our most notorious case was one

involving an exotic cabaret dancer from Florida named Tawny, who was sued along with the club owner by a plaintiff who attended her show. The gentleman had gone to the club as part of a bachelor party and had volunteered to sit in a chair onstage while Tawny plunked her breasts on his head, after which, he claimed whiplash injuries and sued her. Remember, this was at one point a legitimate claim, subject to the Florida courts. We didn't make this stuff up.

Tawny turned out to be a very intelligent woman with a sweet demeanor. She was very large on top, reminding me of Dolly Parton, but tiny below, and she carried herself very professionally. The plaintiff, on the other hand, did not impress me. During the testimony, after he stated that the defendant's breasts were like granite when they fell on his head, I had an idea. I asked Tawny if she would submit to a physical examination by our female court officer, a woman named Josephine. She readily agreed, and the court officer came back and made her report. She said Tawny's breasts were soft and weighed approximately two pounds each. I didn't believe they caused the whiplash, so I found for the defendant.

During our thirty-nine-week production schedule, we taped shows on Tuesday and Wednesday. On those days, as on all other days, I was up at five o'clock in the morning, on the treadmill by six-fifteen, and in my law office by ten after eight. By one-thirty in the afternoon, I'd already put in what most people would think of as a full day, but I was just getting started. I arrived at our studios (initially on Seventh Avenue, opposite Madison Square Garden, and later at Thirty-seventh Street and Fifth Avenue) and started on my second full day. We taped between eight and ten cases a night, one right after another, and were usually at it until nine o'clock, with five-minute bathroom breaks every hour and a half-hour dinner break at five-thirty. During the dinner break, I treated myself to a short nap on the couch in my dressing room "chambers." I've been blessed with the ability to awake refreshed from a short nap. I can fall asleep during a quick car ride and step out energized and rejuvenated at the other end, and I consider this a gift.

My experiences on this set were markedly different from my experiences on any other set. Here, for the first time, I was the key man on the show, and there were about forty people working on the program in various capacities. I don't particularly enjoy "star treatment," but I must say it wasn't all that onerous to have everyone so solicitous of my welfare. Much of the real work was done by the producers, and by the people who found these interesting, unusual cases for us to try on the air. By the time I arrived, the nuts and bolts were all in place, and it simply fell to me to see that the trials were conducted in a professional manner.

The show had an enormous impact, in terms of recognition. When I traveled outside the New York area, I heard far more shouts of "Hello, Judge" than I did of "Hello, Mayor." In New York, it ran about fifty-fifty, but in the heartland of America it was maybe two to one in favor of "Judge." I always told people who referred to me as "Judge" on interview programs that I was really an arbitrator; I didn't want to mislead anyone, but the power of television is enormous.

Years ago, if someone had told me that, at seventy-four, I would emerge as one of the most well-known "judges" in the country, I would have given that person the telephone number of a good shrink. But here I was, just that, and making more money than I had made at any time in my career.

But all good things come to an end. On a

134

Monday morning in March 1999, on my way by car from Boston to the Brandeis University campus for an afternoon lecture, I took a call on my cell phone from Jim Griffin at William Morris. "I have some important news," he said, "but call me when you get to a secure telephone."

I thought, A secure telephone? "Is it good news or bad?" I said.

"Bad, but with a good twist," he said.

Twenty minutes later, from Brandeis, I called Jim back and he filled in the blanks. Stu Billett had called and told him the producers were planning to replace me on *The People's Court*. "Compared with Judge Judy," Jim said, telling me what I already knew, "you're in the tank."

I was surprised but not stunned, and oddly I wasn't disappointed. The twist was that the producers had decided to offer my seat on the bench to Judy's husband, Gerry Sheindlin, whom I appointed to the criminal court and who was planning to leave the real court. The other twist, Jim Griffin reported, was that Stu Billett felt terrible at having come to this decision, and that he wanted to keep me on as an adviser for two years, at an annual salary of $250,000. "He likes you, Ed," Jim explained. "He feels bad."

"That's a generous offer," I said, feeling strangely relieved that my stint playing judge was coming to an end. It would be good to have my afternoons and evenings back, for the two days I was now giving over to taping, as well as the ability to schedule lunches and dinners.

"The plan is for you to finish out the second season," Jim explained, and I agreed that this would be fine. I had no trouble continuing on these terms. We were all professionals.

The next day, I called Stu in California. He was embarrassed, and said he had to make the move to protect the show and its time periods around the country, since our ratings were so low compared with Judy's. I repeated that there was no need to feel bad about it, that it was a good business decision. He asked if I would attend a press conference in the next ten days or so, to good-naturedly pass on the gavel to Judge Sheindlin once all the contracts were signed, and here again I agreed. How could I not agree? The man wanted to pay me $500,000 for what essentially amounted to bowing out gracefully, putting a positive spin on this latest development, and providing assistance for the next two years. Even so, it was a long week or so until the formal announcement, with the press running unconfirmed but accurate stories on what was to happen. When I was questioned on the matter, which was often, I simply answered, "I am not permitted to comment" and referred reporters to the program's press secretary.

When I reported back to work after the Easter-Passover recess, there was no tension or hostility in the air, nor should there have been. I told my own staff back at the law office what had happened, as well as my family, my law partners, and a few close friends, before the story broke in the papers. Most were concerned about my feelings, and worried that I would feel bad at being let go in such a public way. But I didn't mind it at all. "Look how lucky I am," I said. "I've had this opportunity for two years and made a million dollars a year, and I've done it my way, because I couldn't do it any other way." My thinking was, Let's move on to the next challenge!

On April 8, 1999, a press conference was held at the St. Regis Hotel in Manhattan. In attendance were Judy and Gerry Sheindlin, Stu Billett, and Dick Robertson, president of Warner Brothers Television, our syndicator. Dick spoke first and said many nice things about me, which I appreciated. Then it was my turn. I acknowledged that Judy had done so much better in the ratings — her 9 to my 3, each point representing a million people. But I'd had a wonderful time, learned a whole new business, and was paid handsomely for my efforts. Now it was over, and it was time to pass the gavel on to Judy's husband. I felt no ill will toward any of these people.

Stu Billett then made some very nice remarks about the friendship he and I had developed, after which the floor was opened for questions from the assembled reporters. Just three months earlier, WABC Radio had decided not to renew my daily radio show contract, and I was asked how it felt to lose two such prominent media jobs in such a short space of time. I was expecting just such a question and responded with good cheer. "Now I have nine jobs instead of eleven," I said. "Is there anyone in this room who has nine jobs?"

Of course, I got no answer.

I was asked what I would do with my spare time, to which I responded there was no such thing, and that I had no plans to wind down. "I will either get another job," I declared, "or put more time into the jobs I already have. I'll still get up at five, I'll still go to the gym every day, and I'll still stay up past midnight before I go to sleep."

All in all, the press conference came off without incident. Indeed, it was a rather genial affair. "I'm sure the mayor wants to be remembered as the best mayor New York City ever had," Gerry told the reporters, when asked about my legacy.

"Exactly," I agreed.

Then, in a joking manner, Dick Robertson leaned forward to the microphone and said, "I hope I can still get a reservation at Il Mulino," referring to one of the city's best Italian restaurants, where reservations can be hard to come by unless you're dining with a former mayor, or recommended to the owner. Early on in our run, I had introduced Dick to the owner, so he could make phone reservations when others had difficulty.

"Your reservations were canceled last night," I parried.

As of this writing, as I wind down my second and final season on *The People's Court* and look ahead to my continued advisory role with the program, I think of myself as the judicial father of Gerry and Judy, since I appointed both of them to the bench. I wish them well. They've been extremely generous in their comments, and both have spoken of what they consider their debt to me for their judicial appointments. Of course, those appointments were entirely on the merits, as I wrote earlier, but they were grateful just the same.

And I am grateful as well for the chance to push my talents in a new direction. That things didn't work out as planned does not mean they were not worth the effort. In the end, that's the true lesson of my daytime television experience. "Life is not a bowl of cherries," as we used to sing in the forties, but neither is it the pits. It's up and down. We have good ideas and bad. Sometimes a thing works, and sometimes it doesn't. The key, always, is to remain open to possibility, and to remind yourself that if you are going to go up after being down, then you must not allow your mind, body, or spirit to languish.

On the morning of September 16, the day Hurricane Floyd hit New York City, I received a call from Stu Billett.

He said, "Ed, we had to wait for the new season to begin. We now have the money, so I'm going to send the $250,000 to you."

I said, "Stu, that's awfully nice and very generous of you."

He said, "No, it was you who kept the show going for two years, and we are very appreciative."

I thought, he is an extraordinary and honorable individual. I don't believe that there are many people who would have done what he did.

I ended the conversation by saying, "I'm still available. Think of another idea for a show, and let's work together again."

He laughed and the conversation ended.

Life goes on. And on.

five

Sweat and Effort

No primer on remaining relevant into so-called retirement would be complete without a chapter on diet and exercise. Certainly, maintaining the appropriate energy levels to keep active and healthy requires more of an effort as we age — and we tend to pay for our transgressions a bit more heavily with each passing year. In my case, I pay, but that doesn't keep me from looking to cut the cost a little; I love a bargain too much to accept my fate as it first appears.

Let me restate the obvious: I am no athlete. This might be something of a surprise, but I don't come by what I and no one else refers to as my Greek god–like physical fitness naturally, or even easily, at this point. I don't care much for sports. I never have.

There was, at one point, an explanation for this — or, at least, a ready excuse. As a child, I sliced the tendons in my left hand, after running into a plate-glass door during a game of tag. It was a major injury, and it might have left me with a permanently unusable hand were it not for the alertness of my doctor. Nevertheless, 150 stitches and a year of physical therapy later, I ended up with about 20 percent less strength in my left hand, which was now atrophied and visibly smaller than my right. I had a built-in excuse to avoid organized physical activity for the rest of my growing up. Throughout high school, I avoided gym "on account of my hand." I was tall, and people generally assumed I was a good athlete, but I always begged off "on account of my hand." When I was drafted into army service, I did not mention my hand to the doctors during my physical because I was fearful of being designated 4-F. In basic training, I had difficulty with the obstacle course — not directly because of my hand, but because I was out of condition. I corrected that by practicing in the evening after we were dismissed for the day. My brother was the athlete in the family. I was awkward and not terribly well coordinated.

This lack of interest in sports followed me

into my adult life, and even into my political career, where I was sometimes called upon to attend one professional sporting event or another. As mayor, when I had to go to a baseball game at Shea Stadium or Yankee Stadium, I stayed for only the first half-inning, but then my staff pointed out to me that I was being disrespectful to the other team, so I started staying for the entire first inning. More than that, I found it boring. The fans never held it against me, my leaving early; they didn't boo because I didn't feign an interest that didn't exist; they understood that I was there to celebrate the spirit of New York, and not to root, root, root for the home team. I couldn't even tell you the names of most of the players.

I used to ski as a young man, back in the late 1950s, before it became really fashionable. It was a thrilling sensation, to be soaring, birdlike, down the hill, but I was never more than a low-grade intermediate. The last time I went skiing was in 1960. I was at Jay Peak, in Vermont. Each time I came down the mountain, I had the same wonderful, soaring feeling. But after the fourteenth trip, as the snow continued to fall and the hour grew late, I asked myself at the top of the mountain, What the hell am I doing? At the time, I had my own law practice. I didn't have a partner. If I hurt myself, there was no one to take over. I thought, This is nuts. So the fourteenth time was the last time, and I've never been back. I'm told the sport has changed dramatically in the last forty years. I know they no longer use lace-up boots or wooden skis. It's funny how things change when you're not looking.

When I was mayor, my favorite sporting event was the New York City Marathon, in which I took part throughout my three terms. Don't go getting the idea that I actually *ran* the marathon. I merely *participated* in the running — in the same way that Rosie Ruiz *participated* in the running of the Boston Marathon. (Remember Rosie Ruiz? She was the young woman who had the winner's wreath taken from her head after she was found not to have passed certain checkpoints along the course.) In my case, though, I wasn't putting one over on anybody. I used to head out to the Fort Wadsworth base on Staten Island, at the start of the Verrazano Bridge, and mingle with the assembled runners about an hour before the race. The people were always so friendly, and so happy that the mayor would come out early on a Sunday morning to cheer them on. I shook hands with the runners and joked good-naturedly that I'd join them in the race when I left office, when I had time to train. Of course, no one took me seriously. One look at me and they could tell that the day I'd run twenty-six miles would be the day an angry, rabid dog decided to chase me for twenty-six miles.

At the start of the race, I would climb into this wonderful open touring car — a 1952 Chrysler, as I recall — and ride ahead of the lead runners. Fred Lebow, the director of the New York Road Runners Club, was himself something of a showman, and I followed his lead. After all, it was his race. As we snaked along the marathon route about a mile or so ahead of the pack, I'd have the driver stop a couple hundred feet from each water station, whereupon I would get out and start running. I cast myself as the lead runner, and I yelled, "Water! Water!" It was wonderful. The streets were lined with people, six and seven deep, and the last thing they expected was to see their over-weight, middle-aged, casually dressed mayor leading the field. It took everyone by surprise. And they loved it! The people would yell, "Water! Water for the mayor!"

The marathon is truly one of the most spirited, unifying events in the city, and it has only a little to do with sports. Naturally, it's a tremendous accomplishment to be able to run twenty-six miles, and the elite runners are truly phenomenal athletes, perhaps the best conditioned in the world, but my favorite part of the race is the sideshow. It is also, for good or ill, a tremendous political event, because it usually comes around on the calendar about a week or two ahead of Election Day, so you'll often see wannabe or wanna-stay politicians at various points along the course. It runs through almost every neighborhood in the city, every ethnic enclave, and it attracts New Yorkers in droves. It sometimes seems as if the entire city spills out onto the streets, and one of the great aspects of the race is the way the elite runners share space with the middle-of-the-pack and the back-of-the-pack runners. In this regard, it's like no other world-class sporting event I know, and I think that's what people respond to. There was a genuine excitement to those fall afternoons, and I remember drinking my water and climbing back into the open car and shouting, "They're coming! They're coming!" I was like Paul Revere, sounding the alarm.

As a personal goal, however, the marathon held no appeal. I've never enjoyed physical exertion of any kind, and to run a marathon, to spend all that time training, you at least have to enjoy it. A brisk walk was about my speed then, but these days I don't even manage that. Now, because of my enlarged prostate, I don't like to be too far from a bathroom. It's psychological, as much as it is physical. I have a constant fear of being caught too far from a bathroom and having to urinate. Any time I walk past a bathroom I get the urge to go, which I might not have had before. Then it's, Well, if I don't go now, maybe there won't be the chance to go later. I'm aware there are operations to correct my condition, but I'm not crazy about the possible side effects.

What are the possible side effects? Well, I'll place them at the punchline to the following story. I have never been reluctant, since leaving office, to discuss my various medical conditions. I turn them into newspaper columns, or chapters in my books. I discuss them on the air. It's a kind of public service to help take a little bit of the fear and uncertainty out of what happens to us as we get older. There's nothing wrong with it, nothing to be ashamed about. It's part of aging. It was in this tell-all context, after I discussed my prostate on my radio program, that I received a letter from a woman whose husband had just undergone a procedure to correct his prostate condition, urging me to speak with him about it. She felt that since I was so open about my condition on the air, she could be open with me about it in her letter. The operation, she said, was a marvelous success. As it happened, the woman's husband exercised every morning at my gym, but I suppose he was embarrassed about approaching me directly on such a personal subject. If I was interested, the woman suggested, he would introduce himself to me on the next possible occasion and fill me in.

Naturally, I was interested in hearing someone else's war story and seeing if it could in any way be applied to my own, so I looked for this woman's husband at the gym and asked him about his experience. "Oh," he said, "it's just been fantastic. Now I can urinate. I can sleep through the night."

It sounded too good to be true. "Did you experience any side effects?" I asked.

At this, the man was quiet for a moment, and then he said, "Yes."

"What?" I wondered. I knew it was too good to be true.

"Impotence," he said, "and incontinence."

I thought, That's all? It's quite a trade-off, and it doesn't happen to everybody, but a huge percentage of patients experience some level of impotence or incontinence, and in some cases they experience both. Often, these conditions can last for the rest of the patient's life. It's ridiculous. Right then, I decided I would never have this operation. I decided it wasn't so terrible having to get up every morning at four o'clock, for the first of maybe three or four subsequent trips to the bathroom. I considered the alternatives and accepted this as my lot in life. It's an inconvenience, and a constant worry, but as a practical matter it's not a monumental problem. Either it's difficult to urinate, or it's impossible to produce a strong enough stream to evacuate fully, but life goes on. It is marvelous how a human being can adjust.

There was, as I recall, only one occasion when my condition was the cause of a public embarrassment, and I mention it here in the interest of full disclosure, and of helping others who have gone through something similar to recognize that they are not alone. A short time after suffering a stroke in 1987, I was asked to speak at the New York Public Library on Forty-second Street. Thousands of people were there, and all of a sudden, as I stood at the podium, this enormous pressure to urinate just hit me. There was nothing I could do. There wasn't even time to excuse myself politely from the podium to go to the bathroom, that's how sudden the whole thing was, and I actually urinated in my trousers. Fortunately, the trousers were dark, and nobody was aware of it except me, but I was overwhelmed with shame. I've since realized that we shouldn't be ashamed of things beyond our control, but that was my response at the time. I kept on speaking — I was later told that I gave quite a good speech, which I attributed to the fact that I *always* gave a good speech — and as soon as I was through I raced to the bathroom to clean myself up. As far as I know, no one was aware of what happened. I can't imagine that *somebody* didn't notice, but I'm grateful that no one said anything. I'm usually quick with a ready response in almost any situation, but it would have been a challenge to come up with something to say under just those circumstances.

On election night in 1998, I was with Senator Al D'Amato and Governor George Pataki at D'Amato's hotel, where he was taking the returns. I had been a vocal supporter for D'Amato during his reelection campaign, making commercials and public appearances, because over the years he had been a tremendous friend to New York City and a good friend to me. It was only fitting that I join him that night, once his defeat at the hands of Chuck Schumer appeared inevitable, to offer some support and perspective. After all, I'd been down a similar road several years earlier, and I was proof that there is indeed life after political defeat.

What I wasn't counting on, however, was mechanical trouble. I squeezed with about ten other people into a tiny elevator car, as D'Amato made his way downstairs to offer his concession speech, and all of a sudden the elevator stopped between floors. For twenty minutes, we were trapped in an elevator built to accommodate maybe four people. The governor was there, along with his wife, Libby. The senator was there. I was there, and for the whole time I was thinking, Dear God, I'm standing right behind the governor! Please don't let me pee here! Please let me control my bladder! It was the psychological component that nearly did me in because once it occurred to me that I *couldn't* go to the bathroom, it was all I could think about. This time, thankfully, I survived the ordeal without incident, and I wrote about it in my column that week. Every other political wag in the city weighed in with his or her take on Schumer's stunning victory, and I wrote about not wanting to pee on the governor in the elevator on the way down to D'Amato's concession speech.

For the most part, I am able to control my condition, and I've learned to live with it. I take a drug called Cardura to lessen the pressure and allow a freer flow of urine; it's been a successful course of treatment, and I'm prepared to take the drug for the rest of my life. I've even had my agent contact the drug manufacturer, to see about enlisting me as a spokesperson. I figured, if Bob Dole can do it for Viagra, then I could do it for Cardura, but I've yet to hear from them.

Now that I've touched on the subject, let me run a quick inventory of my daily medications, just to give you an idea of the accommodations some of us must make to old age. In addition to my prostate medication, I take a drug called Coumadin, to thin my blood and prevent stroke. It's a very dangerous, very expensive drug, and I'm told it's also used as rat poison. It causes rats to hemorrhage. I sometimes think, if I didn't have such good medical coverage, it would be cheaper to buy the drug from an exterminator than from a pharmacist. Luckily, I've responded quite well to this particular medication, but I have to monitor it very carefully. Every three weeks or so, I go in and have my blood checked.

I also have an erratic heartbeat, called atrial fibrillation. A pacemaker was put in about six years ago, which was recently replaced. I take a number of beta-blockers and other drugs to regulate my heartbeat. I exercise daily, but my results are limited by the pacemaker and the medication. Typically, in strenuous exercise, you look to get your heartbeat up around 110, depending of course on your age and your physical condition. In my case, though, I never get above 72, no matter how hard I work out. The pacemaker controls it. So it's a trade-off. I'm not losing as much weight as I'd like to, because you really need to get the heart pumping to derive a thorough benefit in terms of weight loss, but I'm maintaining a measure of control that in my case is vital, and I've still managed to increase my physical strength.

The most important thing, according to my doctor, is to stay thin. With me, the goal is to become thin, because I can't *stay* thin until I get there. After my first pass at the SlimFast diet, when I lost forty pounds for big bucks, I managed to keep the weight off for five years. I was down to 200 pounds, but I've put back about 25 of those pounds. I'm still fifteen pounds ahead, but it gets harder and harder. That's why I go to the gym.

Even if I don't take the weight off, I at least move it around so it looks nicer.

I'm always on a diet. One of my more recent finds is something a friend of mine spotted on the Internet called "The Mayo Clinic Diet," although it has not been endorsed by the Mayo Clinic; in fact, it has been repudiated by the Mayo Clinic as a fraud. Indeed, there's major controversy among nutritionists over the effectiveness of this diet, but I tried it anyway. It was recommended to me by Mary Barron, whose husband, Bruce, happens to be my doctor. He also happens to be a gynecologist, but he monitors my overall health, much like a general contractor; he refers me to various specialists and subspecialists, as the need arises — not on a fee basis, but as a concerned friend. (Regrettably, or perhaps just inevitably, the need arises more frequently with each passing year.) Mary told me about this diet, and it sounded like the most amazing thing. Every morning, it called for a breakfast of two strips of bacon and two eggs, any style, with butter. On the side, you had to drink a big glass of grapefruit juice. For lunch, a salad, accompanied by as much protein as you wanted (fish or meat), and another big glass of grapefruit juice. For dinner, it was much the same, with still another glass of grapefruit juice. (I didn't need a diet guru to tell me that the grapefruit juice was the key to this plan.) It was essentially a low-carbohydrate diet, with an emphasis on fat and protein, and according to the information that came with the diet, available on the Internet, it was developed for people with heart problems and could help you lose as much as fifty pounds in just three months.

I thought, My prayers have been answered! A friend later suggested the diet should be called the "Hellmann's Mayo Diet," because of its high fat content, but by any name it was just the diet for me. I love to eat, and I especially love to eat bacon and other fatty foods. Bruce Barron, Mary's husband, didn't want me on the diet, but I was determined to give it a try, so I did a little end-around and went to see my internist and cardiologist, Dr. Joe Tenenbaum, a wonderful, extremely understanding man who shared my taste for fatty foods and my distaste for the bland diets that are understandably recommended to heart patients. I told him about the diet, and he was skeptical, but I pleaded my case. "Try it," he finally said, "but don't stay on it for too long." I suggested two weeks, and he agreed, saying, "It won't kill you in two weeks." I had the feeling that if it worked for me, my Doctor Tenenbaum would be the next to try it, since he has a similar weight problem.

So I tried it, and it was terrific. It's easy to follow a diet when it allows you to eat all the things you crave — and in hearty amounts. I lost ten pounds in my two-week trial, which I quietly considered extending to a third week. I felt marvelous, and I had tremendous energy, and I thought, Well, if two weeks didn't kill me I'm willing to chance a third.

Indeed, I was so overjoyed with the success of this diet that I became almost evangelical about it. One evening I found myself at a dinner party seated next to Arlene Alda, the wife of actor Alan Alda. She was very distressed when I told her about the diet. She was aware of my heart condition, and my stroke, and my prostate. I was a well-known hypochondriac, and I told my medical stories the way someone else might talk of a winning game of tennis. "Ed," she said, with grave concern, "you must get off this diet." She explained how the acidity of the grapefruit juice tended to increase the potency of many prescription drugs. "I'm surprised your doctor didn't tell you this," she said. "Grapefruit juice should not be taken with any medication."

Well, that was all this hypochondriac needed to hear. Right there at dinner, I could feel my heart racing, and my blood thickening. I was a dead man, I felt sure. It scared the hell out of me. I quit the diet right away and went to Dr. Tenenbaum for a consultation. He commented on how well I was looking, but I told him how distressed I was to have to give up the diet. I told him about the grapefruit factor. With this, he said, "Let's take a look at the computer." He had a special software program, which allowed him to analyze all the drugs I was taking and measure the impact the high grapefruit-juice intake might have on each. As it turned out, the grapefruit juice didn't affect any of the drugs I was taking. Dr. Tenenbaum knew this when he first allowed me to experiment with the diet, but he wanted me to experience it for myself. So now I do occasionally revert to this diet. I haven't told Bruce Barron, because he'll just have a fit, so let's just keep this to ourselves.

Now, when I return to the diet, I'll do so for a couple weeks at a time, as a kind of refresher course. You've heard of yo-yo dieters? Well, I'm more a pendulum dieter. I swing this way and that way, more than I swing up and down. I lose weight, I gain weight. I try this, I try that. If you had to chart my weight since I started to put back some of what I'd lost on the Ultra SlimFast diet, you'd see it's been fairly steady. In fact, I even go back to the SlimFast diet from time to time. I never stay on it for very long, but I figure a shake here and a shake there is better than no effort at all. My only trouble with it is that it's not the most *social* diet on the scene. A big part of my day is going out to lunch and dinner with friends and associates, and back when I was a paid spokesperson I had no trouble schlepping my SlimFast drinks wherever I went. I put up with the inconvenience, and with what some people might have considered an embarrassment. I brought the shake mix with me to the restaurant and drank it while my friends or colleagues ordered regular lunches. I told waiters to charge me for a full meal. Generally, they wouldn't, but I always made the offer. It made me feel more comfortable about it. Nowadays, I find such a prospect somewhat awkward. When the reward was a lucrative endorsement deal, I had no trouble putting up with some of the social difficulties in following a largely liquid diet, but now that the only things at stake are my health and my life, I seem unable to accept the inconvenience and denial of real food. In the back of my mind, I know I can always return to the SlimFast plan and be successful at it, but I can't seem to find the psychological push to make that total and binding commitment. I'm hopeful the William Morris Agency will return me to the fold, as a product spokesperson, so I can give it another go.

I've found, in my travels, that the ways people diet reflect their personalities. I happen to be a very disciplined person, but at the same time I'm not shy about indulging myself. These two traits do not go particularly well together when it comes to making a concerted effort to lose weight, but they have served me well enough. I can't see giving up *all* the good things in life, simply to prolong that life. What's the point? I eat for sustenance, and I eat for health, but I mostly eat for enjoyment. There are certain foods I crave and will never give up. I can make concessions to age and nutrition, but I can't go cold turkey — which, incidentally, is delicious alongside a warm cranberry-sauce compote and some stuffing. (And don't tell me to avoid the skin of the turkey — that's the best part!)

I don't quite know where my love of food came from, because my mother was not exactly a world-class cook. She burned everything, but it was all I knew. Still, there were certain things she burned well, and I had my favorite burned dishes. One of her best recipes was deep-fried chopped meat, or *hachfleish,* which nobody eats anymore because they're so sure it will kill you. They're probably right, but they don't know what they're missing. My mother used to deep-fry the meat patty in chicken fat. Ah, was that delicious! Absolutely the most wonderful thing I've ever eaten — served hot, in a patty, like a hamburger. It didn't matter if it was burned. Just thinking about it makes my mouth water. She also bought second- or third-cut veal chops. The first cut was like a rib steak, very expensive. One of the things you paid for, with that first cut, was the appealing appearance of the meat. By the third cut, it was so misshapen it looked terrible, but it tasted just as good, and when it was breaded you couldn't tell the difference, and it was cheaper than the better cuts.

A big staple of my diet, growing up and still, is tuna fish salad, which I like to make out of the can with onions and mayonnaise and a little balsamic vinegar, and eat with a tomato. The right tomatoes can be just heavenly. I don't buy American tomatoes except in the summer, when you can find the giant beefsteak kind, since generally they're hard and tasteless, so I buy Israeli or Dutch tomatoes. These are expensive, perhaps $4 a pound, whereas American tomatoes cost maybe 69 cents a pound, but they don't taste any good, so what's the point?

Lately, I eat a lot of Japanese food, although I eat mostly sashimi, rather than sushi. Sushi has too much rice, which is very high in carbohydrates, while sashimi is just the raw fish; for certain diets, yellowtail is the best, for its high fat content. I also eat a lot of salad, and when I cook for myself it's usually rib steak, well marbled with fat. I enjoy a nice piece of fish from time to time (particularly shad, which is in the herring family and fatty), but perhaps not as frequently as I should. For some carnivorous reason, whenever I go to Balducci's, I'm drawn to the red meat case. The way they've got the meat laid out in the counter there, it all looks so wonderful. Plus, it's so easy to cook a steak. Afterward, when I'm cleaning up, I wonder why I was so enthusiastic in anticipation of eating a simple cut of meat, but I must say I always look forward to the next big, juicy steak. It's one of those foods where the *idea* is often more fulfilling and enjoyable than the *reality,* but I keep coming back for more anyway.

My one acquired taste is for anchovies. I love them, as a complement to a salad or on their own. I once mentioned in a television interview that I was in the habit of making myself anchovy sandwiches, particularly when I came home late in evening after a long taping session of *The People's Court*. Now, nobody has ever come out and announced a fondness for anchovy sandwiches, and a few days later I got a letter from some guy in the anchovy business who was so delighted with the endorsement that he sent me a giant tin of his best stuff.

Without mayonnaise, I don't think I could live. (Of course, it has to be Hellmann's — nothing else comes close in flavor.) I add it to almost everything I make, at least to every sandwich, in one way or another. Who the hell cares that it's high calorie? It's allowed on the protein diet, and it's too good not to enjoy. What's wrong with a little fat? I think the way they trim the steaks and lamb chops these days is just a sin. That's the good part! Leave it on! The fat doesn't go on your body as *fat*. That's the mistake people make in forming their diets. A certain amount of fat is good in moderation, but then everything is good in moderation. I just happen to enjoy a whole lot more moderation than most people, at least in this one area.

Exercise has been an integral part of my daily routine since leaving office in January 1990. I work with a personal trainer, for some of the same reasons I've been unable to match my first success on the SlimFast program: I need the incentive to give me the drive to do it. I go to the New York Sports Club, on Fifty-first Street, between Lexington and Third Avenues, where the Sports Training Institute is located. These days, I do about fifteen minutes on the treadmill, then sit on a chair to cool down for fifteen minutes while I wait for my trainer. I used to do a half hour on the treadmill, but I've reduced it over the years. I've added those lost fifteen minutes to the back end of my routine — on the exercise bicycle — so it's not like I've given anything up in terms of cardiovascular conditioning. All that walking just got to be too much for me. It got too boring. Now, I don't like walking faster than three miles an hour, which is not very fast, but that's what I do. For a while, I made up for the slow pace by setting the machine at incline. When I started out, I set the machine at an incline rating of 15, but ten years later I had brought it down to 3.5. More recently, however, I've stopped walking at an incline altogether. One of the most important rules in exercising, I've learned, is to know your own limits. I've learned to listen to my body, and these days it's telling me to slow down and keep the machine flat. It's telling me some other things, too, but I won't go into all of them here.

As I said, after the treadmill, I sit and cool down. In my case, the term is a misnomer, since I don't sweat when I walk. I don't exercise hard enough. But the cool-down is my favorite part. I listen to my Walkman — Andrea Bocelli and Sarah Brightman — and it is one of the great pleasures in my life. I don't much care for exercising, but *having* exercised . . . now that's a wonderful feeling, and it's almost worth the entire ordeal just to have these few moments to myself. It's truly the only pocket of time I allow myself to tune out the rest of the world and just relax. I wholeheartedly recommend it.

After fifteen minutes, my trainer pulls me from my reverie, and we move over to the weights. I work on the machines, and with free weights for about forty-five minutes. I hired a trainer because I wouldn't know what I was doing otherwise, and also because I needed someone to push me. If I didn't have a trainer, I'd be reaching for my Walkman in no time at all. He helps me to set realistic goals for myself, and then to go about achieving them. My trainer is careful to see that I don't hurt myself. The older I get, the more certain parts of my body seem to rebel at all this hard work. My knees are getting to be a problem. I find I'm more aware of them as I go up and down stairs, and we work against this in our sessions. I've also had a rotator-cuff injury, at the back of my shoulder, which required an operation in 1994, but the weight training helped me to a full recovery. I did all the rehab exercises the physical therapist prescribed, and a little bit more besides, and one day the nurse asked me if I was doing more than they were telling me to do. I thought maybe I'd gotten myself into some kind of trouble, maybe I wasn't doing enough, maybe I wasn't progressing as swiftly as I should have been. But I told her the truth. "Yes," I said. "I am."

She said, "It's interesting. People who do more than we tell them to do generally heal more quickly."

I thought, Then why don't you tell people to do more?

Inevitably, my various medications don't always mix with my exercise routine, as happened recently. On Monday, March 22, 1999, I awoke at 4:50 A.M., as I do every day, to get dressed for the gym. I had agreed to meet New York State Comptroller Carl McCall and Bronx Borough President Fernando Ferrer to get arrested together that morning at 11:00 A.M. at One Police Plaza. We were doing this to protest Mayor Giuliani's refusal to meet with the black leaders of our city following the shooting death of Amadou Diallo, an unarmed West African immigrant, by four police officers.

I was not feeling up to par, but my rule is that if I do not feel bad enough to go to the hospital emergency room, I go to the gym. This is a pretty good rule. I'm sure that if I start finding excuses not to go to the gym, I'd find a new one every day.

When I got to the New York Sports Club, the stairs to the second floor seemed especially difficult, but I climbed them anyway. Since I was not feeling my best, I decided to delay my exercise routine by not using the treadmill and wait for my personal trainer to exercise with him. This gave me an extra fifteen minutes to rest. At 6:45 A.M., my trainer, Ed Rhodes, Jr., approached, took my blood pressure and said he couldn't find it, which happens sometimes. Normally, my pressure is a perfect 128 over 70. Strangely, I did not feel nauseated or dizzy, nor did I pass out, which might be expected if my pressure had dropped precipitously. I said, "Let's train anyway," knowing my pressure moves around a lot, which is called "labile," sometimes moving to a low of 90 over 60. I try not to let it stop me from exercising.

But then when I stood up, Ed noticed that I was unsteady and that all the color had drained from my face. Now everyone was concerned, and one of the other trainers, Chris, who was standing nearby, said he wanted to call EMS. I protested but not too hard. Within five minutes, EMS, police officers, and firefighters had arrived. Fortunately, there is a firehouse as well as a police station on the same block as the gym, and everyone was extraordinarily generous, comforting, and supportive.

The EMS officer took my blood pressure and reported that it was 70 over 40. I said to myself, That's almost flat line.

Then he said, "We're taking you to the emergency room. You don't look good. Where do you want to go?"

I told him Columbia-Presbyterian Medical Center, where my internist/cardiologist, Dr. Joe Tenenbaum, has his office.

The EMS officer responded that I was not stable enough to make the trip to Columbia-Presbyterian. "We'll take you to New York Cornell Hospital, at Sixty-eighth and

First," he said, and then added, as if to allay my concerns, "They're affiliated with Columbia-Presbyterian now."

When I arrived at Cornell, the emergency room doctor, Dr. Chang, was extremely supportive without being patronizing or obsequious. My pressure was starting to come back. I told the doctors about the prescription drugs I take for my stroke, irregular heartbeat, and enlarged prostrate. I also told them I had taken a diuretic the day before to relieve edema in my ankles. I had lost four pounds on Sunday. While lying on the gurney, I was thinking, Can I get out of here in time to get arrested? I had too much to do to spend any more time in the hospital.

Former mayor David Dinkins called me at the hospital to ask how I was. I replied that I was fine, but that I was trying to figure out how I could get out in time to get arrested. He had been arrested in a similar protest just a few days before, receiving wide media attention as he and Congressman Charlie Rangel were both placed in handcuffs by the police. He understood the importance of the act, but he still tried to talk me out of it. "Ed," he said, "I don't think you should get arrested today. It's ridiculous." I knew he was right.

I happen to like David. He is genuinely a

very nice person, and I was incensed when he was handcuffed; of course, I publicly blamed Giuliani, saying that the cops would never have done that without his express permission. How awful for New York, I thought, as that picture of two of our major black leaders flashed around the world. While David Dinkins is no Nelson Mandela, he sure looked like Mandela when they put him in handcuffs, and I thought, How harmful this is to New York City's image. It was that image, as much as anything else, that precipitated my decision to get arrested.

I called Dr. Joe Tenenbaum at Columbia-Presbyterian. He said he wanted me to be transferred there because at Cornell they would perform every medical test known to man since they did not know my condition. They'd be afraid to let me out, and I'd likely be there a week, and I could forget about being arrested. Joe told me he had asked Dr. Stephen Scheidt at Cornell to take care of me. At that point, Dr. Scheidt informed me there had been an enormous number of press inquiries regarding my condition. He said there were perhaps a dozen television cameras in the E.R., and that reporters were asking to interview me. "But if you'd like," he said, "we can handle that for you."

I said, "That's fine, but what will you say?"

The doctor said that he'd tell the press I was stable. For New York reporters, that means just one step above near-death. Near-death is "critical," as far as most reporters are concerned. I told the doctors that I would handle the press conference on the way to the ambulance before going to Columbia-Presbyterian. So, I reclined on my narrow gurney, sitting up on one elbow like a Roman senator having dinner — or, at least, how I imagined a Roman senator might look in a scene I recalled from the Masterpiece Theater production of *I, Claudius*.

I explained my condition to the reporters assembled at the hospital. Andrew Kirtzman from the New York 1 cable channel asked, "Has Mayor Giuliani called you?"

"No," I replied.

Kirtzman asked if I found this upsetting.

"No," I replied again, and added, "In any event, I have no intention of taking on the mayor in my weakened condition." Joshing, of course.

The ambulance ride to Columbia-Presbyterian was extremely bumpy. I remember being amazed that they do not have gyroscopes for ambulances the way they do for ships at sea.

At Columbia-Presbyterian Medical Center, I was in the hands of the great internist and heart doctor Joe Tenenbaum, who is most comforting and supportive, but he doesn't baby his patients. He told me that he would take all of the necessary tests and if all was well, I would be home that night. "We'll know by seven P.M.," he said.

I was CT-scanned, X-rayed, and otherwise monitored constantly. I took telephone calls all day. Sometime in the afternoon, Mayor Giuliani called. He was very friendly and asked about my condition. I told him I was okay and expected to go home that evening. Then I said, "I'm going to give you some unsolicited advice. You should meet with Virginia Fields [the Manhattan borough president, who is black]. She is very moderate, much more than I, and it's important for you to do so."

He said, "That's all been arranged by Peter Vallone and is scheduled for this week."

I thought, Now I don't have to get arrested, since the purpose of my nonviolent civil disobedience had been to protest the fact that the mayor had not met with the leaders of the minority community. My second suggestion was for the mayor to ask Virginia Fields to put together a meeting of as many black leaders as she could assemble — her choice — so that the mayor could address every question from every person she thinks is a principal in this conflict. "That will include Al Sharpton," I said, "because I know you will not invite him on your own."

"I'll have to think about that," Giuliani replied.

At 7:00 P.M., as promised, I went home. My doctor said I could resume my normal work schedule the very next day, and my regular gym routine the day after that.

The following Saturday, at 6:00 P.M., while I was lying in bed watching television, expecting to leave for the movies in an hour, I received a call from City Hall. "Is Mayor Koch at home?" the caller wanted to know.

"Yes," I said.

"Can he take a call from Mayor Giuliani?"

"Of course," I said.

Giuliani got on the line. Despite our public criticisms of each other, we are always very civil when we meet privately, or on the telephone. What's the point of being harsh and hostile, when civility is so much more pleasant? "How are you, Ed?" he inquired. When I told him I was feeling fine, he said he had called to ask my advice. Charlie Rangel had issued a statement that Giuliani was not comfortable with blacks and Hispanics and had refused to meet with Charlie over the past year. Giuliani maintained he had met with Rangel many times — at least a dozen in the previous twelve months — on power zones and various other items. The mayor asked me how he should respond.

I said, "A soft answer. Invite Charlie for breakfast, lunch, or dinner, or any other convenient time for him. Say the past is unimportant. Say you want to address the future and meet now."

Giuliani said he was meeting with everyone.

I reiterated my earlier suggestion. "Get Virginia Fields to invite five, ten, maybe fifteen people," I said, reminding him that she would undoubtedly include Al Sharpton, who, I noted, had conducted himself very responsibly in the aftermath of the Diallo shooting.

Giuliani disagreed with my assessment, but he voiced his disagreement softly, not wanting to upset a sick man. He said, "Have you seen the pictures they carry of me looking like Adolf Hitler with his moustache, calling me 'Adolf Giuliani'?"

He was clearly upset.

"Rudy," I said, "it's all street theater. They want to get you mad. And remember what they did to David Dinkins." I was referring to the pictures of Dinkins that the Lubavitcher Chassidim had carried after the Crown Heights riots, with the word "murderer" on the placards. I suggested he stop arresting protesters at One Police Plaza, and instruct the cops to create a path from the curb to the door, so that people could enter the building unimpeded, and let the demonstrators picket without arresting them.

He responded that he had already told them to do that, but apparently the police couldn't find a way. I thought, Nonsense! Giuliani runs the police department, and no cop of any rank would dare refuse his order. "Of course it can be done," I said, and Giuliani agreed he would attempt it again. I told him of a black woman who lives in my apartment building and who, after asking about my health, laughingly admonished me for not having been counted on this issue. "You still haven't been arrested," she playfully reminded me.

In our conversation, Giuliani reported that Jesse Jackson had called his office in advance of his protest, to arrange for his early release from the arrest process. I said to myself, Things are getting out of hand. I was no particular fan of the mayor's, but the slow-footed response to the police shooting of Diallo was dividing the city. He had to do *something*. I told him, "There is a narrow window for you to change things around. You are getting better editorials than you could have expected. Use the time to assuage and conciliate."

He said he would do everything I suggested except for the meeting that would include Al Sharpton. He said he wanted to think about that one.

I tell this story in such detail because I believe it holds two messages. First, God is good — or, as they say in Arabic, *Allah hu-Akbar.* My health is terrific. I have fully recovered. Indeed, my neurologist, Dr. Jay Mohr, at Columbia-Presbyterian, after examining the CT scan of my brain and comparing it with one taken in 1987 when I had my stroke, concluded that my brain was only six months "older" than it had been in 1987. (Back then, when I was age sixty-two, he told me I had the brain of a twenty-eight-year-old.) He said that now my brain has not shrunk with age, as is normal, and still fills my entire skull. I don't care if he's joking, it makes me feel great, which takes me to the second message: I am still relevant. My opinions count. Even my political adversaries seek my advice and appear to consider it carefully, and this is enormously gratifying to me — with each passing year, even more so.

Through all my medical ordeals and various efforts to keep in fighting trim, there's been one thought in the back of my head: Never give up. It doesn't matter if it's a new diet, or a hard-to-keep exercise routine, or some version of the work you've done your entire life. Never give up. Press yourself to do more than you think possible. And if you can't do it by yourself, get some help. In my case, I chose to hire a personal trainer to coax me over the rough spots, but most people can achieve the same success by going to the gym with a friend. You can cheer each other on. Plus, they have all kinds of classes — bicycle classes, aerobics classes, weight-training classes, everything you can imagine. I find that exercising is unique among the intensely personal efforts that most people undertake for purely selfish reasons, in that you can make it one of the least solitary pursuits in your daily routine. And believe me, it helps not to have to go it alone.

At work, there are all sorts of innovative

time-share or mentoring arrangements that might offer an ideal accommodation to advancing age or a reduced level of commitment. There are endless ways to recalibrate your efforts to the point where you are putting in the kind of time you can comfortably manage while still maintaining your position of influence. The key is to try.

Whatever it is, it can be done. I get to the gym early in the morning, shortly after six, and I'm always struck by the people I see there at that hour. There are always twenty-five people, working out, and it's the same twenty-five. It's a wonderful thing to see these men and women carving out time in their busy schedules to ensure that they'll be able to keep those busy schedules for many years to come. Some of them are young, and some of them are old, and in this context I tend to think of myself as old, but only as a measure of comparison. In other respects, no, I can't and won't think of myself as old. Seeing these people there, on a daily basis, encourages a camaraderie to set in. We talk about what we had for dinner, how much weight we're putting on or taking off, how good we look, how we manage. I enjoy the small talk, and the companionship. It puts my efforts in context. I say to myself, This isn't so bad. If I'd put myself in just this picture as a young man, I might have cringed, but at seventy-four, and generally healthy, and active, and relevant . . . it's not bad at all. I've gotten here by degrees. I didn't always watch what I eat. I didn't always have a pacemaker. I didn't always take ten medications on a daily basis. But here I am, and it all seems to be the most natural progression in the world.

I wouldn't have it any other way, although at one time in my life my prescribed lineup of daily medications might have put me off pills altogether, if I hadn't been such a pragmatic person. My parents never took prescription drugs. When my mother died of cancer, at sixty-two, she did so thinking Bufferin had in some way helped her condition. It eased her pain, and she made the leap to thinking it reduced the cancer. Ridiculous, right? But this was how she thought. She didn't like taking drugs. Neither did my father, and that's the way I was brought up. Just as an example, let me tell you one of my mother's earliest homeopathic remedies for the common cold or sore throat. She was of the opinion, learned during her own childhood in a poor Polish village, that a cloth soaked in the patient's own urine and wrapped around the patient's throat was an effective cure for sore throat. I must say, it worked, in the sense that after a few minutes of this you very quickly said, "I don't have the cold anymore! It's long gone." That's how I remember it worked with me. (Or, at least, that's how I choose to remember it!) When your mother tells you to try something, you try something, although I'm happy to report that my mother, who was very smart, turned to more sophisticated home remedies as she became Americanized.

I don't like taking pills, but I have to. However, I won't take any more than necessary, which is why I reject certain popular diets that call for dietary supplements. The only pills I'll take are lifesaving. It's the fuel I need to keep myself going, just as the daily grind of working out is a kind of fuel. Going to the office each day, and working in a meaningful way, is also its own fuel. On those early mornings at the gym, I look around at my colleagues on the treadmill and I realize that we are all in this same soup together. The same fate awaits us all. What sets us apart, and what determines the quality of our lives going forward, is the effort we make for ourselves. Most people appreciate the importance of a sensible diet and a workable exercise routine, which accounts for the high turnout at six o'clock in the morning at my gym. However, not so many people accord the same importance to remaining relevant and active in their professional lives, to challenging themselves intellectually the same way they challenge themselves physically.

But it all goes together. It's all part of the same package, and if you refuse to give up, if you refuse to give in to age or to whatever corporate or professional restrictions you find yourself in, then you're bound to fare better than most. You'll be more active, more involved, more alive. It's the difference between doing the most for yourself or the least, and, believe me, doing the most makes all the difference in the world.

Never give up, my friends, because once you do, you're gone. Or, to turn an old expression, you won't even be able to get yourself arrested.

Six

Gray Matters

We live in a society that has accepted built-in obsolescence. We've not only accepted it, we've embraced it. How many times have you heard advertisers tout one "new and improved" product or another? The suggestion is that newer is better, that what was good enough yesterday is no longer good enough today, and that what is good enough today will no longer be good enough tomorrow.

The implications of such thinking are everywhere apparent. It permeates the culture. For one thing, everything breaks. Have you noticed this, or is it just me? Televisions, refrigerators, cars, furniture, stereo equipment . . . none of these items ever look as good as they do in the store, or in the catalog, and none of them last as long as you expect. I'm old enough to remember when manufacturers built their merchandise to last, whereas now they seem to make it to last long enough to take you to the next innovation.

Regrettably, we apply some of the same thinking to the human being in our society — especially to the person who wants to work. The obsolescence comes in arbitrarily, at sixty-five, at which point, in so many cases, you're out the door. It doesn't matter that you can still make a major contribution; what matters is that the end is perceived as near. Youth must be served.

I don't accept the premise. What was once a mandatory retirement age — reached, in part, to coincide with the availability of full Social Security benefits — has now become *de rigueur* for those at management levels. Federal laws protect workers from arbitrary age discrimination in employment and most workers from mandatory retirement. Furthermore, lawsuits filed to enforce these laws have become commonplace. And yet despite these protections, there is often a kind of pressure exerted by certain companies, or even by those in our communities of similar age and circumstances, for workers approaching sixty-five to consider retirement. The message, spoken or unspoken, is that retirement is good for you, a natural progression, and that the sixty-fifth birthday signals the end of one part of a professional person's life and the beginning of another. If you plan to work beyond that age, you sometimes need to justify your decision or give your employer a projected timetable regarding your retirement. It puts your future contributions up for discussion. Your colleagues begin to think in terms of succession, of how they'll manage when you're no longer around.

One of our most serious societal problems, I believe, has to do with how we look on the notion of work. Too many of us think of work as a chore, done to provide a salary that lets us live our lives. Just think how many times you've heard people speak of their jobs in terms of punching the clock, or marking time, or working toward a monetary goal. To my thinking, the work itself should be the goal, and yet if you convey that you enjoy your work you leave yourself exposed to a strange sort of ridicule. People speak of you as a "workaholic" or challenge the choices you've made in your personal life, or question your motives.

From a corporate or management perspective, there is an economic argument that businesses should be free to make their hiring and firing decisions based on costs, and of course it's cheaper to hire a young gun in his twenties than to keep on an older pro in his sixties. But think of the experience that is being thrown away, the ability learned over the years to make sound judgments and the wisdom of patience. On the flip side comes the argument that it's necessary to make room for younger people, to create opportunities for the next generation, but this strikes me as bunk. To cast aside productive people who have served all of their lives, who still have so much to contribute, who don't want to leave is destructive not only to the individual, but to our society as a whole. It leaves us all diminished.

What's tragic in this equation is that those older workers who are legitimately downsized, or those who leave because of subtle or not-so-subtle societal pressures, are typically cast aside unprepared. We don't get lessons in how to handle ourselves outside the workplace. The majority of us spend our entire adult lives behind the safety of a steady paycheck and a place to put our energies each day. And yet so many of us are cast out without adequate financial provision — or even worse, without adequate medical coverage — that the remaining years, which can be many in number, instead of providing enormous pleasure provide enormous pain. We might feel we still have much to contribute, but in many cases we don't get the chance, and our inquiring, insightful minds are left to atrophy, while the rest of our bodies are quick to follow.

That should stop. I haven't made any kind of cultural study on this, but what I've learned anecdotally is that Asians revere the elderly. In tribal cultures, it's much the same thing. The store of experience and knowledge among older members of the community is considered a societal treasure. We should consider it the same. It's easy for me to pontificate, but if more of us shared these concepts it would be easier to change our environment. I realize, too, that I must separate my own experiences from the mainstream, because my experiences are unique. I'm able to fend for myself, and that's been a wonderful blessing. I have had opportunities since leaving the mayoralty at age sixty-five that few others have been afforded — and even though my leaving had nothing to do with age, it had the same effect.

I believe we should work to shift our thinking, to where sixty-five no longer looms as the end of the working road. It shouldn't even loom as a fork in the road, because simple chronology is no reason to redirect your professional goals or responsibilities. In my own head, after losing the election and celebrating my sixty-fifth birthday, I treated it like any other notch on the calendar. I was another year older, another year wiser, another year more experienced. Interestingly, I picked up speed as I moved along. I kept adding new jobs to my busy schedule. Being needed, and wanted, keeps you alive. I believe that. Now, ten years later, I remain convinced that I *still* have much more to contribute before I draw my last paycheck. I remember early on telling my agent Jim Griffin to think of me as a wasting asset. That's how they refer to oil wells and coal mines on tax forms, and I thought the term applied to me, too. I am, like it or not, a wasting asset. Each year, I'm worth less, but only in terms of what I might earn going forward. Each passing day does bring me closer to my Maker, so each day I truly strive to live and work to the maximum.

My desire to keep working has never been about money, but for some people money is paramount. There's nothing wrong with that. Perhaps they don't have enough to get by. They haven't planned for their future or accumulated a sufficient nest egg, or they want much more than they currently have. I have a different perspective. I have lots of money now, but I didn't have so much during my long life in public service. My top salary as mayor was $130,000, but for most of my public service career, it was substantially less. As a congressman in 1969, when I began my first term, I was paid $60,000. And, when I was first elected mayor in 1978, the salary was also $60,000, so I have lived within fairly modest means for most of my adult life. However, I never doubted that I would make much more money in "retirement" than I did in public office. See, we really don't pay our public officials enough, especially those at the highest levels; fortunately, the lure of public office is such that inadequate salaries don't deter candidates from offering themselves in elections. In my case, having enough money for the balance of my life was never a consideration; what I wanted was to keep finding good reasons to get out of bed each morning other than having to go to the bathroom.

Widespread financial unpreparedness is astonishing, because it's not as if advancing age catches any of us by surprise. It's a fact of life. It's there, all along, and yet we look away from it. I suppose I was the same way, too, for a time. I didn't even think about financial planning until I lost the Democratic primary to David Dinkins in 1989. I had my city pension of $34,178 annually, and my Social Security benefits of $19,299, which together were not enough to support my lifestyle. I also draw a federal congressional pension, and I receive labor union pensions from AFTRA, the television union, and SAG, the movie union, but these too do not yield much.

When you think about it, as I have, the basic cost of *living* is essentially the same, whether you're working or not. In the aggregate, the cost of living can often be reduced, because when you're not tied to your place of business you're free to relocate anywhere in the country. Housing in our big cities and suburban areas tends to be more expensive than in more rural areas — especially in New York City and its surrounding communities. Real estate in the North tends to run higher than real estate in the South. Goods and services, too. Development in warm weather regions, our so-called retirement communities, is more pronounced each year, and modest homes in these areas are almost always more affordable than comparable homes in more populated urban communities. Of course, moving out of New York City was never an option for me, but even without relocating it can still be cheaper to live in retirement. Studies show that most people can expect to get by on 75 percent of their preretirement income, although I playfully wonder how much of that reduction is owing to the reduced prices at "Early Bird" restaurants if you're seated before 5:00 P.M., and movie tickets at senior citizen prices.

What's astonishing, really, is how our perspectives are changing ahead of our realities. According to the U.S. Federal Reserve, the median value of families' retirement accounts was $15,600 in 1995. Clearly, that's not enough for most people to live on, even when coupled with Social Security benefits, which suggests to me that most people refuse to accept the inevitable. Every year, around tax time, we're bombarded with advertisements from financial institutions reminding people that it's not too late to open a retirement account. You can't open a newspaper or turn on the radio without getting the message, and yet some people just tune it out. I always wonder, Where have these people been? They should be opening these accounts in their twenties, not in their fifties and sixties. In this one regard, at least, the government has made it very easy to encourage long-term financial planning, allowing investors to put away pretax dollars and allowing retirement accounts to grow on a tax-deferred basis. The idea, for those of you who've had your head in the sand, is to set aside as much money as you can for a time in your life when your income will be substantially reduced, whereupon the money will be taxed at a lower rate as you spend it. The earlier you begin, the better off you'll be — which is the single best argument I've heard for getting a jump start. Talk to an accountant or a knowledgeable friend immediately, if you need help sorting through the various government-approved plans that are currently available.

My personal investment strategy is this: I save money at every opportunity. I know I don't have the expertise to manage my money in the stock market, in which I have always had faith. Even in 1987, when the Dow Jones Industrial Average dropped to 1700, I stayed the course and kept investing in the market, and as that number as of June 1999 exceeds 11,000, I am elated with the results. I tend to invest the money and make no inquiries of my brokers, except on June 30 and December 31, when I ask the money managers for an accounting. I have always worked with professional advisers I trust, and they put my savings into a balanced mix of stocks, bonds, and mutual and money market funds. To tell you the truth, I never know what my investments are from one moment to the next, unless I have the statements in front of me, but I know that my strategy has worked. I have four different accounts, with four different money managers, on the theory that if one manager misses a trend or an investment opportunity, another will certainly catch it. Lately, with the Dow reaching new highs every week, the financial report dominates the nightly news and I chuckle with appreciation for our capitalist system. Alan Greenspan, Federal Reserve chairman, deserves a medal from the American public for his leadership — especially from senior citizens who invested in the market. I'm in for the long haul.

For the most part, this system works effectively, and it suits me. Lately, it's been hard for any of my managers to lose money, because of the overwhelming growth in the financial markets. Once, at a semiannual review with one of the four brokerage firms with which I do business, I questioned why the account I keep with them earned only about a 4½ percent return, while one of my other accounts generated returns of about 25 percent, and another, a hedge fund, yielded 12 percent. I thought a 4½ percent increase was like losing money in this environment. Their explanation was that the money was invested in emerging markets — meaning in countries like Brazil, Indonesia, and Thailand — which had not kept pace with the economies in more developed countries. They expected that situation to turn around, but it had not done so yet.

I mentioned this conversation to one of my other brokers, who asked, "Why do you want to be in emerging markets? There's enough risk in any investment. Why be there?"

A few days later, I called the first brokerage house and told these brokers I no longer wished to be in emerging markets, and they responded that they had already bought $150,000 in that market since their visit to my office. I said, "Whatever you bought, you bought." I meant it and felt no ill will. But I withdrew all the remaining cash from that brokerage house and transferred it to another one. I didn't do it to punish the original brokers, but to preserve my capital; I was uncomfortable with their strategy.

After three or four months, the emerging markets account had begun to plummet — to where my most recent investment was worth about $50,000 less than I paid for it. The head of the brokerage house came to see me in my office to explain his firm's management of my portfolio. "There may have been a misunderstanding," he said. "Maybe we shouldn't have gone further into the emerging markets without first getting your permission" — which wasn't needed for any investment they made on my behalf. He then offered to make up the $50,000 loss for me, which I thought was rather extraordinary. I'd never heard of such a thing. I have a number of friends, with accounts sprinkled all over the city, and no one's ever told me of a broker who was voluntarily willing to eat the price of his bad advice.

"Absolutely not," I said. "When you invested, you had every indication from me that I had not changed my view, which is that you have total discretion. You didn't invest to lose money. You thought the position would do well. When I called to tell you I wasn't happy in emerging markets, you had already taken the position and you owe me no guarantees, and no monies."

I thought that would be the end of it, but the story found me again on the rebound. Apparently, the head of the firm told the story to one of his clients — a very wealthy friend of mine, who in turn reported it back to me. "I heard what you did," he said, "and I must say, that is highly unusual."

I suppose it was — at both ends. I imagine the brokerage house was trying not to alienate a well-known person such as myself, which might explain its extraordinary offer, but I have never sought special deals for myself. Sure, I love buying my clothes at a discount — but only in sales that are available to the public.

However, the incident was instructive. It taught me that it was okay to have a hands-off approach to investing, as long as you didn't become King Lear and give away total control. It also taught me that, at my age, emerging markets might not be the best place for me to put my money. It's like that classic joke about the old man in the produce section at the grocery store who opines, "At my age, I don't even buy green bananas." Well, who's got time for these emerging markets to emerge? Better to forgo the potential for higher returns in favor of a more conservative investment.

Regarding taxes, I always instruct my accountants to pay the government every nickel it's entitled to. "If there's a question as to whether it's us or them," I say, "give them the money." I don't want any trouble with the Internal Revenue Service. When I was mayor, I worried that the IRS would audit me and find something wrong. I had nothing to hide, but who knew what an audit would come up with? More important, though, taxes are our obligation, and I knew better than most how our municipalities rely on tax money to keep going. I have never begrudged the government taking its share of my income.

Despite my policy of taking the government's position in gray areas, I got a call one year from my accountant telling me we were going to be audited. I said to myself, Who is this "we"? My accountant, who has since passed away, was known as Ziggy — a wonderful, sagacious man, who was also a very good accountant. However, he was not, in retrospect, the best money manager; he always reviewed my stock portfolio and was forever trying to get me out of the market and into CDs, where he kept much of his personal capital; fortunately, I ignored his advice in this area. Ziggy wanted to comfort me because he knew how much I dreaded such a call. "Don't worry about it," he said. "Your tax returns are absolutely okay. We'll take care of everything. You don't even have to be there."

I didn't feel good about this development,

but I trusted Ziggy, and I trusted that we had done the right thing. Six weeks later, Ziggy called to report that the audit turned up an overpayment of $485, which would be returned to me in the next several weeks. It was a random audit, but Ziggy felt responsible for putting me through the ordeal, and told me he was only going to charge me $750 for arguing my case before the Internal Revenue Service. I laughed to myself. I had overpaid by $485, based on Ziggy's accounting, and he was only charging me $750 to represent me!

In the area of medical insurance, I'm uniquely well covered. Unfortunately, my situation doesn't apply for most people, but I'll mention it anyway. Most of my jobs offer health care packages of one kind or another, and at any given time I'll have five or six insurance plans in effect. That's one of the great benefits of having so many jobs. (Another, as I've been finding out, is that if you lose one job there's always enough on your plate to keep you busy and solvent — and well insured.) I don't pay for anything beyond my co-payments, which are reasonable and allow me to see any doctor of my choosing, which for a hypochondriac like me is mighty important. Whenever I go to a doctor, I always begin with a caveat, before I explain my symptoms. "Remember," I say, "I'm a hypochondriac, so whatever I tell you, you should discount it by fifty percent." Typically, the doctor will tell me the symptoms I've described are not at all hypochondriacal, and that I'm unusually attuned to my body's needs.

But I do go frequently to one doctor or another. Why not? I have the best medical care in America. I have six medical contracts, with six different providers. I haven't paid a bill beyond my co-payments in the last ten years. And it's not like I'm getting a free ride. I'm paying for it, in a way. Or my employers are paying for it, through their benefit packages. (In my law firm, I actually pay for my insurance, as does every partner.) The biggest savings of all is the total coverage I receive for prescription drugs. Have you looked at the price of some of these medications? If I had to pay for them myself I'd be spending more than $10,000 annually, but it only costs me $10 per prescription each time, for a three-month supply of each.

Medicare, by contrast, is not the best plan going. There are all sorts of limitations. Medicare doesn't pay for prescription drugs, which I believe is an outrage if not a sin. Across the board, the cost of medical care is outrageous, and to my thinking it's the number-one issue we face in the decades ahead. I am not alone in this thinking, although from the slow-footedness of the various moves toward reform you might think we are in the minority. As our population ages, as people live longer, as the so-called baby-boom generation begins to leave the active workforce, what now stands as a national concern will be an epidemic. The much-heralded Kennedy-Kassebaum law, which allows people to leave their jobs and continue their insurance coverage with personal policies, failed to impose any pricing limitations on the insurance companies. The right to continued coverage was an important step, but if it's not affordable what good is the *right* to coverage? As it is, the insurance companies can simply say, "Yeah, we'll cover you," and they can charge you ridiculous rates that can be as much as 400 percent above what it cost when you were covered as part of a group.

I was so troubled by this gap in the legislation that I wrote to Senator Edward Kennedy, urging him to look into the matter. He wrote back, assuring me that he was aware of the problem and he was working on it.

I thought, Yeah, right. Nobody cares. I don't mean to impugn Senator Kennedy on this issue, because he's certainly done more than most, but at bottom it's every man for himself. There are forty-three million people in this country with no medical coverage of any kind. In 1963, that number was thirty-five million, and in a few years it is expected to reach fifty million. And yet the voices of these forty-three million are hardly heard. What do you think would happen in this country if forty-three million people suddenly took to the streets? There'd be a revolution. There'd be rioting, bedlam. Frankly, I don't understand why the unions haven't gotten behind this matter in a bigger way. I'm even surprised that the conservatives haven't seized the issue as their own, instead of opposing national comprehensive health insurance at affordable rates.

Perhaps the biggest culprits, though, are the very people who make up the largest group affected by the problem — the elderly. The main problem I can't get past is that the elderly haven't done more for themselves. *We* haven't done more for *our*selves. If we're as powerful politically as it's widely presumed we are, if we're willing to vote as a block and torture politicians, as it's widely believed we do, then why haven't we been able to achieve national comprehensive medical insurance, including nursing home and home care coverage as well? Why haven't we been able to push the right buttons? I'm not suggesting that we should be irresponsible, or that politicians should respond to irresponsible demands, but adequate medical coverage, with prescription drugs, should be far more readily available than it is. It should be a given, in our culturally advanced society — as, in fact, it is throughout most of Europe.

As far as planning for long-term health care or catastrophic illness is concerned, here's what I've done. I followed my sister's lead and took out a long-term health care policy. She and her husband had recently taken out coverage for long-term, in-home, or nursing home care. It's very expensive — mine costs about $13,900 per year — but I take the premiums in stride. One of the advantages of having so many paychecks is that you can earmark your efforts for specific expenses. When you place the cost in such specific terms it doesn't really seem too bad, and to my thinking it's well worth it, whatever the price. Nursing homes, no matter how well run, have for me the smell of death. There is no question, those who enter them shorten their lives. I hate to generalize, and I don't want to get into a public battle with individual nursing home owners who might indeed offer exceptional facilities, but it's not a fate I can see for myself. I'd never want to be a burden to my sister, or to my nieces and nephews, so I arranged for coverage that offers a substantial allowance for at-home care. If the time comes when I'm unable to live at home, then a nursing home becomes unavoidable, and the policy covers these costs as well. This last item is essential. I hope I never need it, but the cost of nursing home care has gone through the roof. To afford a nursing home often means becoming Medicaid-eligible. This means that people have to spend down their assets, which doesn't seem just. The cost of such care should be incorporated into our national comprehensive medical plan — when it finally takes hold, as I believe it must. Until then, this policy seems like a bargain to me. If you can afford it, I encourage you to look into it.

Naturally, what works for me won't necessarily work for you, but you do need to spend some time on these matters. There is no one "correct" plan to see you through your golden years, but you do need to have a plan. Any plan is better than none at all. You need to consider where your money is going to come from, if you stop working; you need to think about long-term medical care; you need to consider estate planning. As much as I believe that the government is entitled to its share, and that the public interest is served by estate taxes, I also believe that we owe it to our heirs to work within the tax laws to provide the maximum bequest for those we love.

I always tell people it's never too early to start thinking about retirement. If you haven't yet begun to save, start now. If you've already started saving, save more. Most financial planners I've consulted recommend an aggressive approach to funding your pension accounts — *whether or not the contributions are tax-deductible*. Even if you can't invest pretax dollars, the money will compound on a tax-deferred basis, so you will do well to put away as much money as you can to work for you. Find a money manager you trust, don't act on stock "tips," and save, save, save.

Hand in hand with personal financial planning needs comes the increasing worry over the health of our Social Security program. Recent studies suggest that by 2019, Social Security trust fund revenues will cover only three-quarters of benefit costs, and that by 2029, the fund will be depleted if it is not changed. That's just thirty years, which is about the time that many Americans now expect to retire. A recent Gallup poll showed that 90 percent of working Americans believe they will *not* receive full benefits upon retirement; further, 26 percent believe they will receive no benefits at all.

I find these numbers enormously troubling, as I suspect most people do. There's no question that our Social Security program is in need of drastic reform. The latest proposal from the Clinton administration, which includes postponing the age of full benefits, is a step in the right direction, and we have already done this to some degree. Under the current system, the full retirement age will be increased gradually until it reaches sixty-seven. These changes will start in 2003, and affect everyone born during or after 1938. Here again, this is a long-due first step, but we need to look actuarially at contemporary life span tables, and recalibrate them against what it used to mean to be old in this country. Look back to 1935, when sixty-five was truly *old*, and determine what the comparable age might be today. Is it seventy? I don't know. My mother was an old woman at the time of her death, and she was only sixty-two. I'm twelve years older than she was when she died, but I don't think of myself as old and I certainly don't look or act old. I also feel certain that there is no reason to lose sleep over the relative viability of our Social Security program. It will not go bankrupt. Before that happens, the government will fund both Social Security and Medicare out of the general treasury.

As I stated at the outset of this book, I will never retire. The term has no meaning for me. My sister retired, and she's having a good life, and I don't think anybody could or should convince her to the contrary. I tried, but she was right. She retired because her husband had retired, against his will, let go by his employer, and she wanted to extend his life by keeping him company, and she has, no question about it. It works for my sister and her husband, and what I've learned, by their model, is that it's possible to make a life in retirement. That is, for most people, it's possible. For me, no. But it should be a voluntarily embraced condition. I dread the day when I have to try it on for myself, and pray that day never comes. Until then, I'll keep working, because as the title of this book states, I'm not done yet!

People call me a "workaholic." "What do you mean?" I ask, when I hear the phrase. Does it mean I like my work? Well, then, the answer is yes. Guilty, Your Honor. If you think there's something pejorative about liking your work then the problem lies with you, not with me. You don't like your work; you consider work to be onerous, an imposition. I'm not compelled to work. I love my work. I tell people who don't like their work, "Get a different job. One that attracts you. So that when you wake up in the morning you look forward to it." That doesn't mean, at the end of the week, that you don't look forward to a weekend away from work. But not to think of work as enjoyable is anathema for me. It should be a pleasurable part of your life. Sadly, that's not true for many, many people. In my case, life and work have intertwined, they've melded, and I can't imagine it any other way.

True, there are other ways of looking at it, I'm aware of that. I'm also aware that I might look at things differently in the future. Will my financial needs change as I get on in years? Absolutely. Will I have to slow down somewhat in my professional life? Most likely. I joke that I intend to die at my desk, but the reality is that at some point I will have to take on less. I'm not the Energizer Bunny. I can't keep going and going and going, and I won't fool myself into thinking that I can. (I might try anyway, but it won't be out of foolishness.) The question for all of us, though, is, will we slow down by choice? People are "forced" into retirement for all kinds of reasons. The push can come from employers, co-workers, friends, or family members. Or it can come from within yourself. Whatever choice you make, or whatever choices are made for you, it's essential to have a plan. You have to try to be financially secure enough to live an independent life. You need to understand, for yourself, what you're hoping to get out of that life, and what you're prepared to do about it.

I have, and so can you.

Seven

Second Chance

I never let go of a good idea. If it occurs to me once, it will occur to me again, and in time I'll usually be able to persuade others of the merits of my view. Occasionally, a good idea will come to me a little ahead of its time, but I still won't let it alone; eventually, I know its time will come. Even my critics will tell you I'm a relentless advocate of causes I believe in, or of legislation I believe deserves a fair hearing. Some say it as a criticism, but I take it as a compliment. Would *you* mind if someone called you relentless? (I didn't say *ruthless!*) I certainly don't — especially when it's that very quality that often gets results.

I'd like to share with you an example of my so-called relentless nature, and I offer it here because it nicely illustrates some of the themes and values at the heart of this book: Never give up; never back down; if at first you don't succeed . . . and so forth. Strive to matter, and to make a difference. Do your best. These are not platitudes but rules to live by. Remember, I'm not done yet, and here's one way I've been using my energies to affect change, and to stay relevant.

It's a story long in the making, and the ending hasn't written itself just yet, but let me start at the beginning. When I left the U.S. Congress, I came up with a proposal that I thought was unique — and very much needed. In the late 1970s, one out of four black males between the ages of twenty and twenty-nine was either in jail, on probation, paroled, or awaiting trial. These young black men were caught in the criminal justice system — and, once in, many found it difficult if not impossible to rebuild their lives. That figure has grown over the years, so that it's now one in three; worse, in cities like Baltimore, the number of young black males with a criminal record is one in two. It's a sad fact of life that the opportunities available to young men in our inner cities are not what they could be; there are fewer jobs available for young black men than there are for young white men, and even fewer available for young black men with criminal records.

I considered these statistics, then and since, and kept coming back to the related statistic that a high percentage of those young black males were in the prison system for nonviolent crimes, such as drug abuse. I asked myself, Can anything be done to give these young men a fresh start after serving out their terms? I am now persuaded that some of the disparity in the numbers of blacks in prison compared with whites is the product of racism — not all, but some. It's a devastating blow, on a societal level, to have one out of three young black men struggling to make a decent, honest living during their most critical earning years with a felony record haunting their every day. I remember reading surveys suggesting that young women were reluctant to marry young men with criminal records. Why? These men couldn't get good jobs. They couldn't support a family. Often, they couldn't sign an apartment lease, or apply for a loan. They were handicapped, in a very real sense, by the mistakes they had made. In many states, they couldn't even vote. It was as if, once they were caught in the system, they were trapped by it, and no amount of rehabilitation could help them turn things around.

The more I thought about it, the more I

realized we were creating a pariah class of individuals, and I felt strongly that we should do something about it, or it was only a matter of time before many of these young men wound up back in jail. And even if they managed to build a law-abiding life, odds were likely it would be a hardscrabble existence.

When I left Congress in 1977, there were some harsh laws on the books (both federal and state) regarding the possession of hard drugs, many of which remain in force. As the use of crack cocaine became more widespread, the penalties for possession of small amounts of the drug, intended for personal use, became harsher still. The gap between the minimum sentences for crack cocaine, the drug of choice for young blacks, and minimum sentences for the use of powder cocaine, the drug of choice for young whites, was widening. Under current law, first-time offenders convicted of simple possession of five grams of crack cocaine are subject to a mandatory minimum sentence of five years. Yet, for powder cocaine, possession of five hundred grams is required for the same mandatory sentence of five years. Longer sentences are imposed for possession of larger amounts of the two drugs with the same 100:1 ratio being applied. Efforts made over the years by the Federal Guidelines Commission on Sentencing to remove the differential or reduce the disparity in sentencing were rejected by both the president and Congress. Nobody wanted to be seen as being soft on crime, and therefore nobody was prepared to redress a societal wrong. Five years is a long time to subtract from a young man's life, and it's difficult for him to get his footing after being incarcerated for such a long period, so I tried to think through a program that might help set things right a little bit.

Over time, I came up with a plan, and by the time I left the mayoralty I gave it voice: a second-chance proposal, aimed at creating a federal jobs corps for nonviolent felons, who would receive a stipend for the work they did while in the program. Participation would be on a voluntary basis, and participants would be required to get their high school diplomas and learn a job skill. At the successful completion of the one- or two-year program, with an additional year out of the work program but subject to regular drug testing, participants would be eligible for a presidential pardon, provided they had not gotten into any further confrontation with the law and that they continued to test clean. The purpose of the pardon, if Congress enacted the appropriate legislation, was to permit the criminal record to be expunged, so that participants could honestly respond on job applications that they had never been convicted of a crime, and hopefully move forward with their lives: a second chance.

Of course, we have two penal systems in this country, one at the federal level and one at the state level, and the largest number of people are in our various state systems, so individual states would be encouraged to participate in the second chance program, with the governor providing the pardon and the state legislature having the role of Congress. The states could send former convicts to the federal jobs corps or create their own programs. I thought back to President Franklin D. Roosevelt's Civilian Conservation Corps (CCC) in the 1930s, which people my age remember and extol. It was a wonderful program that took Depression-era young people in need of jobs out of their environment and trained them to be foresters, road builders, and national park workers. But my plan envisioned an urban model. I didn't want these young people to be transplanted to a rural, backwoods environment; I wanted them to contribute to their own communities, and to begin to build a life that they could sustain on their own. Of course, the more idyllic model of the CCC wouldn't be rejected, but I thought it best to present the plan in more realistic terms.

When you have a bright idea such as this one, the first thing you do as a legislator is attempt to convince others of its viability. In or out of Congress, a proposal is nothing without support, so I put it out there in the best way I knew, but for some reason I couldn't get a favorable response. (Hell, I couldn't get any response at all.) The political climate was such that there was hardly any interest among public officials in advancing the proposal. This surprised me, I must admit, but I found that the successful far-reaching rehabilitation of nonviolent offenders was not a front-burner issue to most of the people I contacted, and it had to do with the fear that it might be perceived as not being tough on crime. The appeal of the plan, I thought, was that it did not reduce criminal sentencing and kicked in only *after* the sentence had been served. True, it called for a degree of compassion for the nonviolent felons who would qualify, and it's clear the time had not yet come for people to feel compassionate about the plight of these young men. It's possible too that some legislators were put off by what they might have seen as a racial component to the plan, in that the black community, with the largest percentage of eligible offenders, would benefit the most. It's also possible that black leaders did not want to call attention to the problem.

For all of these reasons then, and for others I probably didn't even consider, the proposal went nowhere. I thought, What a shame! What a missed opportunity. It was a troubling outcome to what I believed was a win-win proposal, but I knew that in time I could find support for the plan. Every year, young black males were being arrested and incarcerated at alarming rates, and sent back into their communities with the deck stacked almost completely against them; and by the mid-1990s, after just a few short years of this worsening trend, I felt the time was right to revisit the matter. I began writing letters to everybody I could think of who might have an interest in the idea. I sent letters to members of the congressional black caucus, to the National Association for the Advancement of Colored People (NAACP), to the director of the President's Crime Prevention Council. The response, at first, was disheartening, but I kept at it. I am a persistent letter writer. I make it very difficult for a person not to answer me. I keep writing, enclosing my original correspondence for ready reference. And if that doesn't work, I'll write again. And again. I'm never rude, in these follow-up appeals. Just persistent. Over time, elected officials have come to know that I often publish my correspondence on public issues, if possible with their reply attached, and this last effort usually brings a response of one kind or another.

Typically, I'd hear back that this *still* wasn't an issue anybody wanted to take on. Myrlie Evers-Williams, Julian Bond, and Kweisi Mfume of the NAACP all indicated that the idea had merit, but that it didn't merit being added to their agendas. I couldn't understand it. What could be more important than giving back to our urban communities a chance for their nonviolent felons, under the right circumstances, to start their lives anew? That these nonviolent felons happened for the most part to be young black males only made the cause more compelling, in that it compounded the other difficulties they faced every day because of racial discrimination, and yet I found myself getting nowhere.

Finally, after several years of frustration, I reached out to Charles Ogletree, Jr., a Harvard Law School professor who came to some prominence after representing Anita Hill in the aftermath of Clarence Thomas's Supreme Court confirmation hearings. I met Ogletree at a seminar and started thinking of him as a potential ally. I was always looking for allies for my various causes, and here I'd found a man who seemed to share my concern in this one area. I told him my idea, and he immediately saw its merits. I said, "Maybe you and I could join together and get the support of some of our black leaders." I thought perhaps that one of the reasons I was being rejected in my letter-writing campaign was that the black leaders I was reaching out to resented that some "smart-ass white former mayor" was swooping in with a cause like this one. Maybe it needed to come from within. Maybe if the idea came from me *and* Ogletree, a respected academic who happens to be black, we might get a supportive response.

The professor agreed that this was a matter worth pursuing, and we developed a strategy and refined the proposal to include an ancillary national "scouting" program, akin to the wonderful 4-H program, available to all children beginning at age five, with an emphasis on inner-city communities. This, I felt, was a thoughtful component to the plan, aimed at setting these kids off on the right path, before they had a chance to stray. We sent out a series of joint letters, to Ogletree's contacts and mine, as well as to people with whom we had no personal relationship but who nevertheless were in positions to move our proposals forward.

"The statistics bearing upon the state of the disaffiliated black youth are horrendous," we wrote in a January 1995 letter to Donald Payne, chairman of the congressional black caucus. "It is clear that many of these youths, particularly those with criminal records, will be deprived of future opportunities, including rehabilitation, unless they are given a second chance." We concluded the letter by urging Payne to embrace these two initiatives as the major social programs put forth by the black caucus in the coming year. "We believe that conservatives and liberals, Republicans and Democrats alike, would see both of these programs as eminently responsible and doable," we wrote, confident that we would finally get somewhere.

But once again our efforts stalled, and I began to think, in jest, that Professor Ogletree and I were so far ahead of our time that we wouldn't live to see the positive results of our efforts. Still, I was unshakable in my belief that our proposal — or, at least, some version of our proposal — was the right thing to do, and that it would eventually command the national attention it deserved.

Professor Ogletree and I remained on good terms, and we agreed to let the matter sit until we could find another opening. I was prepared to wait for a better opportunity, if that was what it took, and I believe I finally found it, in the fall of 1998, in the unlikeliest of places. I was a guest on an interview program on BET, the black entertainment cable channel, on a panel with the Reverend Al Sharpton, one of the more outspoken, controversial leaders in New York's black community. Al Sharpton and I had something of a tense history, dating back to the first months of my administration as mayor. He was twenty-three years old, and he came down to City Hall with about twenty-five other black ministers to demand $50 billion in reparations for slavery; the group also sought an increase in the number of summer jobs to be offered to New York City youth, from 55,000 to 200,000. They asked that I immediately sign a petition supporting both demands. I appreciated

Sharpton's concern on the jobs issue and would have preferred to provide as many jobs as possible, but at the time the city budget was on the brink of bankruptcy and could not expand the existing federal program. And the reparations proposal wasn't something I would support. I didn't believe in it then, and I still don't. Indeed, I'd always felt that the near $6 billion spent on the Great Society programs to end poverty were a form of reparations, however misdirected. I even said, as mayor, that if we had given these monies to the poor instead of creating programs for the poor, the poor would be rich.

Sharpton wasn't prepared to wait. He was the kind of leader who wanted what he wanted when he wanted it. He insisted I read his petition and sign it then and there. I wanted to avoid further confrontation, so I said, "Why don't you leave the petition and I'll read it and get back to you?"

"No," he said. "You'll sign it now."

With this, I replied, "This meeting is over," and I stood to leave the Blue Room, the large room at City Hall where we held our press conferences and conducted public meetings.

Sharpton would not be denied. He and three other ministers followed me into my office area and announced they would stage a sit-in until they received my signature of support for their demands. I thought perhaps it was 1968, instead of 1978.

"You can't do that," I said. "You can picket to your heart's delight outside on the steps of City Hall, but not in here."

Still, Sharpton and the other ministers refused to move until I signed their petition. They became an illegal public nuisance, blocking ingress and egress to my office, so I turned to one of the police officers at the scene and said, "Get rid of them."

(Incidentally, under Mayor Rudolph Giuliani, it's no longer possible to picket freely on the steps of City Hall. What a mistake! When you deny the people the right to public protest, you create the kind of police-state atmosphere that should be a politician's undoing. With me, people could always picket. It was a point of pride. More than that, I not so secretly enjoyed it. What's not to like? It's fun. It's street theater. It's New York. In 1967, when I was a councilman, taxi drivers picketed my home at 14 Washington Place because I would not agree to vote for a fare increase unless services were simultaneously improved. I went downstairs and brought the cabbies coffee. I thought it would catch them off guard.

There must have been about twenty-five pickets, and they all carried signs, and they all got hot coffee. Some of the messages on those signs were outrageous, and some were on target. I remember walking up and down the picket line, saying, "This sign is no good. This one's clever. This one is unfair. This one's okay." It was all in the spirit of healthy debate.)

The cop at City Hall looked at me like I had just told him to confront an angry mob, which this certainly was not. He whispered to me, "What if they resist?"

"What if they resist?" I mimicked. "Have you never heard the word 'arrest'? Arrest 'em!"

Indeed, the four ministers were arrested, whereupon I was denounced by the black community as a racist pig. How dare I arrest these black ministers? How ridiculous. There were no exemptions to observing the law. We all live under the same laws. If you want to engage in nonviolent civil disobedience, then you have to be prepared to accept the consequences. You can't say, "Oh, gee, I'm going to violate the law," and then when the law is applied to you, in sanction form, go out and whine that you're being discriminated against. "Oh, don't arrest me!" "Oh, don't punish me!" It was the silliest thing I ever heard, and I wouldn't allow it in my administration. In fact, I sent an order to all the commissioners, instructing them that if their offices were ever illegally occupied they were not to debate the issue. They were to call the cops and have the protesters arrested.

The difference between me and Giuliani in this regard is that I let my critics have their say in the appropriate arena — in the Blue Room, at meetings, outside City Hall, on the streets of New York City. Let them shout all they want, until they lose their voices. That's their right. But it's against the law for them to block ingress or egress, and disrupt the orderly flow of business, and I meant to uphold that law. Giuliani, however, doesn't make the same distinction. He doesn't see that there's ever an appropriate time or place for anyone to protest his actions.

Over the years, as Sharpton's influence grew, I began to see him in a different light. He was still too incendiary for my taste, but he was growing into his role. For years, I didn't like much of what he did, or much of what he stood for, but it was clear he had an important role to play in racial matters in New York City, as a genuine leader in the black community. Indeed, his large vote totals in the past mayoral and U.S. Senate campaigns, primarily in the black community, confirmed his place in city politics. Several years into his transformation, he called and asked me to lunch. It was after his second mayoral campaign, as I recall. He said he was now going to take the road of Jesse Jackson and not the road of Louis Farrakhan. It was certainly the far better road, given the alternative, and I agreed to meet with him.

I have a very liberal policy on accepting meetings, when asked by a New York City public official or civic leader in the relative mainstream of his party. I believe I have an obligation to make myself available to those who seek my advice on matters relating to the city. Nothing is more important than a good dialogue, especially between adversaries.

As my lunch date with Sharpton came around on the calendar, I began to hear about it from friends and associates who would have had no reason to know my plans. David Garth, my longtime political consultant and friend, called to tell me that the word was out all over the city about my lunch with Sharpton. "He's telling everybody," David warned. "He's turning it into a political event."

I immediately called Sharpton and canceled the lunch. "You've done something here which is unacceptable," I said. "You called to ask me to lunch, and I accepted, but you're turning it into a media circus. We're not having lunch."

He didn't get upset. He didn't deny contacting the press, and he didn't try to talk me down from my position. He simply apologized, which I thought under the circumstances was the classy thing to do. I accepted his apology, but I still wouldn't have lunch with him. The damage had been done, and to meet with him in that kind of atmosphere would not have been in my best interests.

As Sharpton became a fixture on the New York scene, people began to look past his flamboyant tactics and his various missteps, including his infamous support of Tawana Brawley and the fraud she perpetrated, and statements he made that reasonable people could construe as antiwhite or anti-Semitic. Gradually, he became a real force in New York politics. He received more than 80 percent of the black vote when he ran for mayor, and he outpaced Liz Holtzman in the Democratic primary for the U.S. Senate, and his statements have become far more low-key on hot-button racial issues. I found myself thinking in terms of his potential as a leader who could span racial diversity. I still disagreed with him on a number of issues, but I disagreed with quite a few viable leaders on a number of issues, and if he could somehow acknowledge, apologize for, and distance himself from some of his past positions I felt he could play an important role.

There was a time when I thought Jesse Jackson was anti-Semitic, but there was no denying his place on the national political stage. He certainly made statements that were anti-Semitic (who can forget his infamous "Hymie town" remark?), but over the years he has changed. Most important, he denounced anti-Semitism in the black community in an Op-Ed article in *The New York Times*, allowing other black leaders to weigh in publicly against anti-Semitism.

Jesse Jackson's not perfect, but I'm not perfect either, and neither is Al Sharpton. Al Sharpton has never been rabidly antiwhite, or rabidly anti-Semitic, the way he is sometimes portrayed. I see his potential. When I'm criticized for meeting with him, which often happens, I refer people to the most recent Anti-Defamation League (ADL) report on anti-Semitism. It says that 53 percent of Americans are not anti-Semitic, but 47 percent are, to some degree. Am I supposed to stop talking to the 47 percent? The report also says that 9 percent of Americans are *rabidly* anti-Semitic. Those people I won't meet with, or seek to involve in a common cause.

It can all get a little foolish, the way we're so quick to write people off. You could take a similar survey and ask people what they think of Greeks or Hispanics. "What do you think of Italians?" "What do you think of blacks?" You could ask the same questions they ask in the ADL survey, and you'd likely get back comparable results. Obviously, there's a large antiblack quotient in this country, just as there are anti-Hispanic cohorts and anti-Italian cohorts and anti-Greek cohorts. Regrettably, it's the nature of our society. What are we supposed to do, stop talking to each other? I prefer to believe that by talking to you I can convert you — or at least reduce your hostility. Of course, there are limitations. There are some, like Louis Farrakhan and David Duke, who are beyond the pale. But it is important to take the higher road and not insult such people, even when making clear our contempt for their actions and statements. I believe Pat Buchanan fits this description, but I would not hesitate to shake his hand. I don't believe shaking hands is anything more than a social grace, and in a civilized society there must be room for social graces, even among the fiercest of enemies.

Certainly, Al Sharpton and I were not the fiercest of enemies. We weren't even enemies. We just found ourselves, from time to time, on different sides of an issue, but there were also times when we were on the same side. There's nothing wrong with that, and as I sat with him on that interview program I thought perhaps I'd found the ally I'd been looking for. The more I thought about it, the more I wondered why the pairing hadn't occurred to me sooner. Sharpton has a very good sense of humor, and a quick mind, and the back-and-forth between us on the program was quite enjoyable. I liked him, personally, and before the program even ended I thought to myself, I'm going to ask him to get involved in this second-chance proposal. I had pretty much exhausted my black leaders on this issue, but more than that Sharpton also appeared well positioned to help me get results. He was, at once, my last and best hope.

After the show, I took Sharpton aside and explained the proposal. He listened intently. I've always thought that one of the hallmarks of an effective leader is the ability to listen, and Sharpton listened well. He asked salient questions and caught what I was trying to accomplish straight off. He even seemed to share my frustration in trying to move the proposal forward. At the end of my pitch he allowed that the second-chance concept was a sound idea, well worth pursuing, and he wondered why other black leaders hadn't been quick to accept it as a priority. I gave him some of my theories: It was perceived as soft on crime, it was backed by yours truly, and so on.

"I'll go back and talk to Jesse," Sharpton finally said, meaning Jackson. "If he likes the idea, the three of us can work on it."

I thought, And Jesse too? It was more than I'd hoped for.

Sharpton phoned me in my office a few days later. "Jesse loves the idea," he said. "Let's get to work on it." He explained that what helped to persuade Jackson was the endorsement by Charles Ogletree, a man of great status in the black and academic communities. No matter how we came by it, his support was meaningful.

"Let's have lunch at the Four Seasons," I suggested to Sharpton. "It'll make quite a stir."

And it did. A couple of days before the lunch, Sharpton called to ask me about the press. He didn't want to get in trouble with me again, but he thought surely we would want some coverage, to generate attention for the proposal. I said, "Absolutely, bring them on!" The difference between this lunch and what was to have been our first luncheon meeting some years earlier was that here we had the same agenda; previously, it had been a case of Sharpton looking to advance his own agenda on the back of my willingness to meet with him.

Sharpton showed up dressed immaculately. He really makes quite an impression when he walks into a room, especially at a staid venue like the Four Seasons. Physically, he's a very impressive man, with his huge head and shock of hair. He no longer wears his trademark medallion, I'm happy to report, but he wears fine tailored suits and comes across as someone who clearly cares about his appearance. As the expression goes, he fills the room with his presence.

We were joined at lunch by Jim Gill, who happened to see Sharpton's name on my daily schedule and asked if he could attend. He had never met Sharpton and was intrigued by him. A lot of people are intrigued by him, and I took Jim's interest as reinforcement that Sharpton's involvement would be helpful to our efforts on behalf of this second-chance proposal. I called Sharpton's office to see if he had any problem with Jim tagging along, but he was fine with it, as I knew he would be. Jim Gill is one of the most respected attorneys in the city, and Sharpton knew he would do well to impress him.

Sharpton can tell a story like nobody's business. When he laughs, which is often, his whole body seems to shake, and the room along with it. It's more of a roar than a laugh. He told us about a conversation he had with Jesse Jackson, just prior to our meeting. During the conversation, Sharpton shared with Jackson some of the things I had said to him when we met on the television program, and in subsequent conversations on the telephone. "You're a leader," I had said, "but you're only a black leader. If you want to become the kind of leader who transcends race, you've got to admit error. You've got to apologize for all of the terrible things you've done, and cleanse yourself of your past." I said these things to Sharpton not as a condition of our partnership on the second-chance proposal, but because I liked him. I wanted to help him. I'm a firm believer in offering unsolicited advice to people who don't always ask for it themselves — particularly when it's me offering the advice.

According to Sharpton, Jackson responded to a secondhand version of my advice by saying, "You listen to that man. He knows what he's talking about." He told Sharpton that he used to dislike me himself — referring, I presumed, to the 1988 presidential race, when I denounced him on national television for his actions surrounding the assassination of Martin Luther King, Jr. Jackson was in the habit of telling people that he had held King in his arms as he died, but it had been widely reported that after King was shot Jackson took off his shirt, bathed it in King's blood, and then put it back on. I read that version of the incident in *The New York Times* and cited it in a televised debate during the campaign.

Jackson's wife was with Jesse and Sharpton when they were discussing me and the second-chance proposal, and at this point in the conversation, according to Sharpton's account, Mrs. Jackson turned to her husband and said, "The reason you don't like Koch is that he told the truth about you."

With this, Sharpton fairly roared with laughter. Soon Jim Gill and I were roaring right along with him. I thought it was a wonderful barometer of the kind of man

Sharpton had become, that he could be so blunt and frank and funny about such a potentially explosive issue. It was almost as if he were telling a joke about himself.

At the end of the lunch, Sharpton and I agreed to get together for another meeting, this time with Charles Ogletree in attendance, to plan strategy. The press was waiting for us downstairs, and we got some very nice television coverage, and a positive write-up in *The New York Times*. I started getting phone calls from other leaders, and reporters. One call stood out — from a reporter writing for *The Forward*. His tone was more eviscerating than inquiring. He asked, "Are you trying to make Al Sharpton kosher?" I thought it was a funny line.

"Yes," I replied, "if he does what I suggested to him."

Ogletree joined us for our second lunch, on a Saturday afternoon at Balthazar, a wonderful downtown restaurant on Spring Street. Sharpton had never been there, but I told him it was the *in* place in town; he'd fit right in — and he did.

Once again, he asked, "Do you want me to call the press?"

"Of course I want you to call the press," I said. I don't normally like to schedule a "working" lunch on Saturday, which is when I eat with my friends of thirty years, many of whom served with me in my administration, but one of the reasons I thought to schedule the lunch at that time was to take advantage of the slow weekend news schedule. I knew full well that the best chance we had of receiving wide coverage would be on a slow news day.

By the time we arrived at Balthazar, there were four television cameras set up in front of the door. I was delighted. If *I* had called them, they wouldn't have shown, but Sharpton was able to bring them out. He's a lightning rod for media attention. Have you ever noticed, whenever there's a tense racial situation brewing in New York City — and, unfortunately, there's often a tense racial situation brewing — that he's in the middle of almost every news photo? I couldn't command that kind of attention. Maybe as mayor, but not anymore. So the press came out, which I thought was wonderful. Public issues require public attention. As I walked into the restaurant, I had another one of my "relevant" moments — thinking, Ah, to be seventy-four and still able to draw media coverage to an important issue. True, the reporters may have come out because Sharpton called them, but they showed up in larger numbers because of the unlikely alliance between Sharpton and myself.

At the lunch, we came up with a plan to stage a conference on the matter, in an academic setting, preferably at Baruch College or Fordham University. It would be on a Saturday morning. We would invite many of the people Sharpton knew and many of the people Ogletree knew, which was many more than I knew. We'd bring out the black leadership and air all sides of the issue, and attempt to form some sort of working coalition. At one point, Sharpton stressed that the conference should be an invitation-only affair. "We don't want the crazies," he said, and I had to laugh, thinking how far he'd come since we first crossed paths.

The key, we agreed, was to remind people that the program we were proposing was not soft on crime. The purpose, really, was to get people back on the right track, after the lifetime of drug use and petty crime and poverty that landed them in the system in the first place. If this will get people off drugs and into a productive life, there's no good argument against it. That's the way we planned to sell it, and we left Balthazar that afternoon confident of our success.

The resulting conference, held at Baruch, was attended by about 150 people. All five

New York City district attorneys sent representatives, who participated in the discussion and offered support. Federal Judge John Martin spoke in support of the concept, as did Eliot Spitzer, the newly elected attorney general of the state of New York, who designated one of his staff members to work with us to formulate appropriate state legislation. All in all, it was a positive response to a positive program that stands to have a far-reaching, positive impact on the young people of our state. Interestingly, not one of the city's daily newspapers mentioned Al Sharpton's important role in this event.

The lesson here, as in many of my endeavors since leaving office, is that we are all cogs in a big wheel. Without the power of elected office behind us, few of us can get anything done on our own, with rare exceptions. But if you put enough cogs together, you have a wheel. And that's what I've tried to do, here and elsewhere. I've recognized my limitations and worked within them — better, I've stretched beyond them. I've sought alliances with people who agree with me on a particular issue, even though on the face of it we might have very little in common. Sharpton and I are as unalike as two people can be, and yet I believe we are both dedicated to helping people. We're both in this thing for the greater good, not for ourselves, and in that we walk on common ground. In truth, we wear some of the same stripes we wore twenty years ago, at our first contentious meeting. Sharpton himself made the point to journalist Sam Roberts, on his New York Channel 1 interview program. He said that if he were to stage a sit-in at my office today, I would have him arrested — and he's right, I would. He also said he wouldn't hesitate to sit in if he thought that was what the situation called for. I thought it was a very clever, very accurate take on how far we've come without really straying from the values that called us to public service in the first place. We've changed over the years, but we haven't changed our basic character, our basic conscience, the way we look at the world. "Even though he had me arrested," Sharpton said incisively, "he never stopped talking to me."

Change doesn't happen all by itself. Good ideas need to be helped along — and sometimes that help must come from unexpected sources. Clearly, I don't mean to suggest that you should be open to working with anyone, on anything. That's a judgment call. You don't work with Adolf Hitler. You don't work with a Farrakhan or a David Duke. Al Sharpton doesn't need me to maintain his position in the black community. If anything, his association with me could be seen as a negative in this regard, among black radicals. But the association may help him to expand his position in the whole of our society. He may gain respectability in the white community. I understand that. He understands that. We've talked about it. Here, on this one issue, we found a way to come together to make a difference — and, hopefully, it's about to make all the difference in the world.

Eight

In Good Conscience

Human beings are social animals. There have
been all sorts of experiments to demonstrate
this point. Left alone, we fail to thrive. The
exchange of ideas, the warmth, the compassion . . . these things are all tremendously important aspects to a fulfilling life.

I could never understand how people
manage to work full time, at home alone,
and not in an office with other people.
Forget for the moment the rewards of a
challenging career. It's not *just* about the
work. It's also about the people. At a certain
point in our lives, I suppose it's even *mostly*
about the people. It's about getting out, and
interacting, and feeling as if you are an important piece of a greater whole. As it was
for my father, it's about having a place to go

each morning, something to look forward to, a reason to get out of bed.

I know that there would be a tremendous void in my life if for some reason I stopped working, and I can't imagine how I'd fill it. I can't imagine how I'd grow — socially, culturally, ideologically. I worry that I'd be like one of those monkeys in experiments, wasting away in isolation, or becoming neurotic. I worry that my thinking would become stale, that my days would be empty, and that those days would be numbered. It's a worry that most of us share in one way or another, but we all act on it in different ways. Or we suppress it, and make the kinds of decisions that move us from the fast track to the slow lane, from relevance to irrelevance, from a rich, full life to no life at all.

You know, it's funny, but I've never fully imagined how my career will slow down, or when. I suppose it will someday, but I'm not looking forward to that day, and I have no wish to think through what my days will look like at that point. I've had glimpses, and I don't think I've liked those glimpses. I was truly distressed when I lost my radio job, and I was disappointed when I lost my *People's Court* television job, although it was not as wounding. I simply plowed forward in the other aspects of my career and assumed I'd fill the extra time with other jobs that were equally challenging, or devote more time to my remaining nine jobs. And I have. However, I'd be fooling myself to think that this will always be the case, and so I don't. I might will it so, and I might put up all kinds of public defenses to suggest that a fate such as this will never find the likes of me, but I know the truth.

Someday, I know, I won't be able to replace one gig with another. Already, it's not so easy. It's been nearly a year since I lost my radio show, as I set these thoughts to paper, and from the looks of things it does not appear I'll be able to replace that situation with another just like it. Happily, I can still find other productive outlets for my energies, but I can't seem to replace *like* with *like*. I miss the show itself, the doing of it. I miss the way I had to read the papers each morning, the immediate connection I had with my listeners. It was like no other job I ever had. There was instant feedback, and a feeling of being plugged in that I simply don't get from my other jobs. As I wrote earlier, it was a lot like putting out my own newspaper each morning, with the distinction being that unlike the traditional newspapers, I attacked and criticized my competitors for their editorial opinions or lapses in reporting on a regular basis.

I still relish this feeling of connectedness, and I pray it never leaves me. While I tell my agent to think of me as a wasting asset, at the same time I know I'm a valuable resource. I look at the upcoming candidacies of people like Al Gore and Hillary Clinton, and I see there's a role I can play. I've endorsed Gore before — I supported him for president in the 1988 New York primary — but I don't think I will endorse him again. I don't think he can win. I think he is going to be just like Hubert Humphrey, who lost the 1968 presidential election because of the Vietnam War. Humphrey, then vice president, could not attack President Lyndon Johnson for his position on the war, and there are many who feel that's why he lost the election. I was there when Humphrey was asked about why he wasn't more critical of President Johnson, and he responded, "Where I grew up we don't piss in the well from which we drink." He could not, having been treated well by Johnson, attack him. And I don't believe that Gore will be able to be critical enough of President Clinton, and that's why he will lose. People are fed up with Clinton, his lying and his lechery and his betrayals, but Gore's not going to be able to speak freely on the subject. Even if Gore could, he might alienate a whole other group of people by doing so, so I really see him in a no-win situation. Gore is a man of character, and yet he will be forever saddled with Clinton's vices. Of course, there will always be those who will wonder, quite reasonably, why he couldn't tell the difference between a Buddhist nun and a bonded messenger from Goldman Sachs (referring to the campaign money scandals), but that's another matter.

With respect to Hillary Clinton, there are some who see me as a kind of key to her prospective U.S. Senate campaign, especially if she runs against Rudy Giuliani in the general election. I don't happen to see myself as a key, but I can understand the view. I have such a distaste for Mayor Giuliani, and people know this. If you think about it, I'm in a unique position on this matter. Because of my connection with New York voters, and because of my outspoken opinions on her likely opponent, I will undoubtedly be sought out, if and when she runs. As this book goes to press, she has yet to announce her formal plans, but she did call me, before taking her trip to Egypt and after I had written a column urging her to run. She thanked me for my public remarks and asked for my views on various issues, and I like to think I can take some of the credit for her recent candor on health care reform.

Tellingly, I heard from Vice President Gore on the same day I received my phone call from the First Lady. He had read comments attributed to me that I might support former New Jersey Senator Bill Bradley in his run for president, and he wanted to let me know how disappointed he was to learn I was no longer in his corner, since we were such good buddies. "Perhaps we should get together and talk," he said.

I thought, You walked away from me in 1988 — when I was still mayor, and supporting you for president over Michael Dukakis — because Jesse Jackson didn't like me or appreciate my attacks on him.

He then said, "We have to get you down to the house," meaning the vice president's residence in Washington, and the invitation seemed disingenuous. He'd had six years to invite me down, and hadn't thought to do so until I made my statement regarding Senator Bradley. As it was, the invitation didn't hold much appeal. I'd already seen the vice president's residence: Nelson Rockefeller had invited me to a bash when he and his wife, Happy, were the tenants.

Naturally, the endorsements of former politicians have always been sought by current politicians, so I don't consider this particular form of relevance as being all that meaningful. It's a fact of political life, and I accept it. I enjoy it, and I take my responsibilities in this area quite seriously; however, I much prefer the kind of relevance I can generate on my own.

Here's an example: the murder of a young man named Matthew Shepard out in Wyoming, during the fall of 1998. It was a horrible incident, and by all accounts Shepard was murdered simply because he was gay. I wrote a column about it for the *Daily News*, maintaining that the gay political action groups attempting to enact hate legislation were perhaps misdirected. I said that such legislation was not as important as some might think. The idea of hate legislation is that if you commit a crime that is racially motivated, or motivated by homophobia, then the penalty should be greater. Murder is murder, and the existing penalties for murder are sufficiently severe. I can understand how in so-called bias crimes you must give extra weight and attention to apprehending the perpetrator because of the larger impact on society, but for the most part I don't think hate crime legislation will contribute much toward reducing these crimes. What would be even more helpful, I wrote, is what I was able to achieve here in New York as mayor, which was to prohibit by law discrimination in employment and housing based on sexual orientation. That legislation was passed in New York City in 1986, and I'm very proud of it. It took a long time, and a lot of effort — and, bizarrely, the law has no counterpart at the state level in New York and doesn't exist on a federal level.

After the column appeared, I wrote a letter to Senator Joseph Bruno, the majority leader in the New York State Senate, in which I suggested that, based on the Shepard case, he let his conscience guide him on this matter on the state level. "I have great admiration for your fundamental decency," I wrote, and asked if he would allow a conscience vote on the legislation introduced by Senator Roy Goodman adding sexual orientation to the categories protected from discrimination in housing, employment, and places of public accommodation. I reminded Senator Bruno that such legislation was passed in New York City in 1986, and that those who opposed its passage in the city council, when asked by the media on the tenth anniversary of the 1986 legislation, said that they would support it today, given the opportunity. I pointed out that at least a half-dozen other cities or counties throughout New York had provided comparable protection, but most of the state was without it. I also noted that the Shepard incident had caused many governors and legislators throughout the country to rethink their opposition to comparable legislation. I reminded Bruno that the state assembly had passed the legislation year after year, but supporters had never been able to bring it to a vote in the Republican Senate.

Bruno wrote back, thanking me for my letter and saying that he was not prepared to bring the matter to a vote at this time. He did say, however, that he remained open to a discussion of the issue.

I immediately called the sponsor of the legislation, Roy Goodman — a Republican, a friend, and a very decent and able legislator — and I told him about this. He told me that Joe Bruno could not let it come up for a vote because the Conservative Party was against it, and Bruno needed the support of the Conservative Party for his members. So I called Mike Long, the chairman of the Conservative Party, who had been in the New York City Council with me a number of years ago. We are also friends. Mike is a very conservative man, but also a man of conscience, and I brought him up to speed on the issue. He laughed and said, "I bet they told you I was the man who was stopping this."

"That's true," I said. I then suggested that even if he was homophobic, he had an obligation to let the matter come to a vote.

"I'm not homophobic," he insisted. "I don't agree with the legislation. I don't understand it. But I don't hate people based on their sexual orientation." He then paused a minute and wondered aloud, "Why don't they let the vote prohibiting partial-birth abortion take place in the assembly?"

With this, a lightbulb flashed over my head. It seemed such a simple, workable solution to the impasse that I wondered why it never came up before.

I'm not an ideologue. I support gay rights and I also support ending partial-birth abortion. Generally, someone who supports gay rights is also in favor of partial-birth abortion. Somehow or other, those are liberal icons — and, of course, the reverse is true of conservatives. In fact, the Conservative Party points to my support of ending partial-birth abortion in all its letters, and I've encouraged it to do so. I said, "Take out an ad. Have it say 'Even Koch is against partial-birth abortions.' " So we have a good relationship on this issue.

What a wonderful idea, I thought. A quid pro quo. Conscience votes on both issues. I told Mike he might have something here, and promised to get back to him on it as soon as possible.

I then wrote to John Cardinal O'Connor, with whom I also enjoy a good relationship — we even collaborated on a book together, titled *His Eminence and Hizzoner*. In this letter, I urged the cardinal to support the sexual discrimination legislation, on the basis of hate-the-sin, love-the-sinner, which has always been the Catholic Church's position. Back in 1986, he had opposed the legislation in New York City, although lately he has taken the position that while the Church would not take an active role in the matter, it would not oppose similar legislation, provided that the Church's immunity from such legislation remained intact.

Cardinal O'Connor called me back and informed me that even before my letter arrived he had already set in motion a series of calls to the state senate indicating that the Church would not object to such a vote.

Next I wrote to Sheldon Silver, the speaker of the New York State Assembly, and I put it to him plainly. If Mike Long was able to secure a commitment from the state senate for a vote on a bill affording equal protection for gays and lesbians in employment and housing, would he commit simultaneously to allow a vote on a bill banning partial-birth abortion? You have to give something to get something, right? That's how it's done all the time in Albany, and in legislative bodies all around the country. And what were we asking these two legislative bodies to give but the chance for a majority vote and majority rule?

He's an interesting man, Sheldon Silver. He's an Orthodox Jew, and when he first ran for the city council, I couldn't support him because he was against abortion and against gay rights. I liked him, but I wasn't about to help elect someone who was so diametrically opposed to my views on these matters. Well, he has changed vastly since then, because as the speaker, elected by a liberal caucus of Democrats, he has to be supportive of gay rights and abortion, no matter what his religious beliefs. I don't know how he's reconciled it in his own head, but occasionally I'll bring it up to him and he'll just laugh. Yet even a changed man cannot always see his way clear to a just solution. Why shouldn't people have a right to vote to ban partial-birth abortion in the assembly, where Sheldon Silver refuses to put it on the calendar? And why shouldn't people have a right to vote on gay rights in the senate? The logic, fairness, and symmetry seemed obvious to me.

I then took the matter one step further. I wrote to assembly leaders like Dick Gottfried, chairman of the health committee, and Deborah Glick, a leader in the lesbian community, who were in positions to move my proposal along, and I took up the notion of a quid pro quo conscience vote at every opportunity. "Do let me know," I concluded my appeals to various senate and assembly leaders, "whether you are willing to take the appropriate action to make it happen." And as I signed off on each letter it occurred to me that I was doing just that — taking appropriate action to make something happen, using my position of influence to affect change, to do the right thing, to keep others on their toes.

Regrettably, Sheldon Silver never answered my letter; Gottfried and Glick both refused to support my proposal, but I remain optimistic that something good will come from this initiative. What choice do we have but to be optimistic in our extra efforts?

One more example of my involvement in matters of relevance: In Maryland, a young

American named Samuel Sheinbein was charged with murdering another American, and fled to Israel claiming asylum from extradition back to the United States. Why? Because he was considered to have Israeli citizenship — derived from his father's citizenship, although the young man had been born in the United States — and under a 1972 Israeli law, its citizens were protected from extradition to any other country to stand trial.

I was outraged, as were a great many other Jews and non-Jews around the world, but especially here in the United States. I wrote to a host of Israeli leaders warning of a loss in American support — not as a threat, but as a reality check. I was aware that many countries had similar laws in effect, but this case was different. Israel had always pointed to its special relationship with the United States, and not to extradite an alleged murderer — a U.S. citizen who had allegedly committed the murder in the United States — was unacceptable.

One such letter was sent to David Bar-Ilan, press secretary to then Israeli Prime Minister Benjamin Netanyahu. David wrote back saying that he too was appalled, and that the matter only confirmed that Israel, like the United States, had some bad laws on the books — and some stupid judges, too. Months later, I got a telephone call from David, informing me that the Knesset, the Israeli parliament, had changed the law, so that in the future sanctuary would not be available under such circumstances, and such alleged criminals would be extradited. Lamentably, the law was not made retroactive, and Sheinbein would not be returned to the United States (he would be tried for murder in an Israeli court), but the point was made. A wrong had been righted. "You did it," David said.

Of course, that wasn't true, but I certainly helped to focus Israeli attention on the issue with my letters and column. I should mention here that my dedicated opposition to Israeli extradition laws did not end with the Sheinbein case. In March 1999, I conveyed my views directly to Prime Minister Netanyahu, after reading a *Daily News* article reporting that a resident of New York, accused of defrauding the U.S. government of tens of millions of dollars, was fighting extradition from Israel to the United States. In my letter, I denounced Israel's position in no uncertain terms and called for a rescinding of the 1972 law, which has provided fodder for the anti-Semites of the world. "This is totally unacceptable," I wrote, "and can only cause Israel to be mocked and scorned worldwide as a place giving refuge to Jewish criminals. That would shame every law-abiding Jew in the world, and I do not doubt that it would cause enormous problems for Israel as a result of diminished moral, political, and economic support from countries such as the U.S.

"Would you grant sanctuary to an Israeli Arab or Jew who committed a terrorist act in the U.S. if he were successfully able to flee to Israel? How would you distinguish this case from the one involving the two Libyans alleged to have murdered the passengers on the Pan American flight over Lockerbie, Scotland, who were for years protected by Libya's Colonel Muammar al-Qaddafi?

"It would not surprise me," I concluded, "if an effort were made in the U.S. Congress to penalize the Israeli government by reducing or eliminating economic and military aid now provided to Israel by the U.S. taxpayers."

One month later, I received a reply. "Israel will not allow itself to serve as a haven for criminals," Netanyahu wrote, explaining that the Israel Ministry of Justice had drafted legislation that would provide for the extradition of Israeli citizens, and that a proposed bill had been approved by the Knesset Judiciary Committee.

"I hope this case will in no way reflect on Israel's relationship with the United States," he closed. "Our shared commitment to the independence of the judiciary and to the principle of due process exemplifies the common values which form the basis of our friendship with the American people."

And then, before signing off, the prime minister added the kind of delightful remark that makes the sustained back-and-forth on matters of conscience so worthwhile — and enjoyable. "Let me add," he wrote, "that I appreciate very much your input and concern. I even manage to squeeze a peek into your columns once in a while."

Sometimes a just cause needs an advocate, and I'm always happy to try to do the right thing. It's why we social animals are here in the first place: to make the world a better, fairer place. To keep ourselves alive, and active, and contributing, for as long as we possibly can. Understand, I care about the linking of these two contentious issues, and moving them forward in our state legislature, and I care about the unfair asylum offered by Israel to an alleged American murderer and an alleged American embezzler. I care about remaining in the mix. If it's not gay rights or partial-birth abortions or a refusal to extradite to the United States an alleged criminal charged with committing a crime in the United States, it will be some other set of issues. There are always other issues, other causes I will take up as my own. Sometimes I succeed in my initiatives, and sometimes I don't, but the initiatives keep coming, and they fill my days and keep me feeling young, and alive, and plugged in. They keep coming, and I keep at them.

It's what I do. It's what I've always done.

Nine

Age Gracefully (or Die Trying)

Have you ever noticed how those in the public eye must sometimes go through their pivotal, life-changing moments on a public stage? Even nothing special, business-as-usual moments are up for inspection. If you collapse at the gym in the early hours of the morning, it's immediately on the news. If you're fired from your job, it's written up in all of the city's papers. If you're seen having lunch or dinner with someone with whom people don't expect you to be seen having lunch or dinner, it, too, is reported in the media.

I've been in the public eye for over thirty years, and while I honestly don't understand why I'm still the subject of media comment, I'm inured to the lack of privacy. I don't think about it or let it dictate where I go, what I do, or what I say. It comes with the territory. More often than not, I'm followed by shouts of "Mayor!" or "Judge!" — not only on the streets of New York but in the airport of any large city. I don't know which is more startling, that people remember me from my two-year stint on *The People's Court*, which ended in May 1999, or that they remember me from my twelve-year run as mayor, which ended a decade ago.

Sure, the attention is often just plain fun, as long as it's offered in a positive way. If I notice people looking at me, scrunching up their faces as if they're not sure it's really me, I'll usually call out, "Yes, it's me." They invariably smile. If it's clear they recognize me and they greet me, I always say, "Aren't you nice." I'm truly appreciative of the many kindnesses that continue to be shown to me.

Those who know me well will agree that I am not by nature an introspective person. Nor am I particularly outgoing. When I tell interviewers that I am actually shy and retiring, they always laugh. Their laughter is never meant to be insulting, but to convey their opinion: "Boy, are you naïve!"

When I lost my radio job at WABC, or more recently when I was "benched" by *The People's Court*, I couldn't avoid collecting comments and commiserations from friends, colleagues, and perfect strangers, and there's no better distraction from disappointing news than the well-wishing of others. It's not a cure-all, but it's an effective palliative, and it offers a built-in sounding board to help you sort through whatever it is you're feeling about your situation.

There's another benefit to all this public inspection, and that's the way I've been allowed to listen in to what other people are saying about me. It's almost like being around to hear your own eulogy. I'll hear or read some comment about my contribution to the city, or what I've come to represent to New Yorkers, and inwardly I'll think, I've really been lucky in having had David Dinkins and Rudy Giuliani as my two immediate successors because they've both made me look good. They've instilled in New Yorkers a kind of nostalgia, a longing for a more comfortable past. On occasion, particularly if I'm in the news because of a health-related incident, there is an underlying tone to these reports, as if to suggest, Well, he'll soon be dead. Obviously, a visit to the emergency room at age seventy-four is regarded more gravely than a visit to the emergency room at sixty-four, or fifty-four. I expect to live to eighty-seven, my father's span of life. I am a fatalist by nature, so I'm not overwhelmed by my visits to the hospital before I reach that age. If God takes me before, I'll not hold it against Him. He has been very generous to me.

What also comes with having lived a public life is the way a public flap can resonate in a positive way, and here I look to two recent Giuliani-fueled incidents to make my point. It's funny how public perception of a series of exchanges can differ so dramatically from your own firsthand view, but I find the contrast instructive. Both stories centered on the City Hall's Blue Room, the public room adjacent to the mayor's office, which in the fall of 1998 was slated for refurbishment. As part of the renovation, I learned in a December 4 account in *Newsday*, Giuliani ordered the removal of two portraits — one of myself, and one of David Dinkins — thereby setting the scene for a colorful back-and-forth between myself and the mayor.

Perhaps the story needs a bit of setup. During my administration, I had begun the tradition of displaying the official portraits of our modern-day mayors in the Blue

Room, beginning with Mayor Wagner. Prior to my term, the practice had been for each mayor to give to the city an official oil portrait, but I was never a fan of the paintings. I appreciated the history, and what the portraits represented, but the paintings themselves were uninspiring. They often looked like paint-by-numbers efforts. I chose instead to donate a photographic portrait of myself, taken by Gregory Heisler, which had appeared in *The New York Times*, although before I could do so I had to convince the Municipal Art Commission that the photo would last as long as a painting, the standard being at least three hundred years. Now, thanks to Rudy Giuliani, it appeared it would do so shielded from public view.

Throughout Giuliani's first term, the Blue Room was decorated with portraits of Wagner, Lindsay, Beame, Dinkins, and myself, along with earlier mayoral portraits from the nineteenth century. So I was somewhat surprised to receive a call from a *Newsday* reporter informing me that my portrait had been removed, along with Dinkins's. I had assumed my picture would hang there indefinitely. I responded, quite reasonably, that there is limited space in the Blue Room, and that the mayor was free to decorate the room in whatever manner he chose. "It's his prerogative," I said.

David Dinkins was less forgiving, and I admired him for it. "The mayor is apparently altering tradition," he said. "If there's space for pictures of the city, then obviously there'd be space for the portraits."

I agreed and devoted my next *Daily News* column to the subject, using Giuliani's actions in this one regard as a barometer of his actions in others. "On reflection," I wrote, "David Dinkins and I are lucky that Giuliani didn't decide to cast our portraits onto a bonfire along with the First Amendment, which he seems to enjoy violating regularly with his denial of parade permits, demonstrations and even the holding of press conferences on City Hall's steps." In recent weeks, he had silenced his critics on a variety of issues by denying them an appropriate public forum in which to air their views. I complained that he had rendered City Hall virtually off-limits to the public, despite the fact that it was the seat of our city government, and compared his reign to the days of the Roman emperor Caligula.

"I am nevertheless amused," I concluded, "knowing that what goes around comes around. In my mind's eye, I see the next Democratic candidate for mayor emerging from the primary in 2001 and asking Dinkins and me for our endorsement. I also see us asking, 'Where did you say you are going to hang Giuliani's portrait?' "

The reference to Caligula was intended partly in jest, but I really felt the comparison was not far off the mark. Rudolph Giuliani has a legendary inability to tolerate criticism of any kind, and it must have rankled him to have to confront the visages of his two predecessors, and his two harshest critics, on a daily basis. Traditionally, if you decided to remove two portraits, you would do so on a "first in, first out" basis, which meant that Wagner and Lindsay should go ahead of myself and Dinkins, so I took it as a transparently venomous act. It's possible I was reading too much into the situation, but I didn't think so — and I still don't. I was also aware that when you complain publicly about a small matter such as this you leave yourself exposed to criticism. (Speaker of the House Newt Gingrich complaining that President Clinton made him leave Air Force One from a rear exit comes to mind as a good example.) A reporter called to pursue the matter, and I merely offered my commentary on it. It was only later, after the story had been picked up by news outlets all around town, that I thought to devote a column to it, and I did so at that point only because I saw it as part of a pattern. It was a story about Giuliani, not about me. It was about how his power as mayor had gone to his head. It was an illustration of his character, his viciousness, his inability to tolerate criticism. That's why he has built a wall around City Hall, figuratively and factually, to keep the rest of us out.

It reminded me of one of my proudest moments in public life. It was 1971. I was a member of Congress, and the Quakers were picketing on the steps of the House of Representatives, reading the names of the American war dead in Vietnam from *The Congressional Record*. It was, many will recall, a very effective and moving form of protest. Speaker of the House John McCormack ordered the Capitol police to have the protesters removed, and the Quakers sent around a letter to every member of Congress, asking for support. In response, I called the speaker to take up their claim. "Mr. Speaker," I said, "you shouldn't prevent these people from reading the names. They have a right to be there."

"Oh, no," McCormack said. "Nobody has a right to be out there on those steps, for any reason."

"But that isn't true," I countered. "Every day, the Boy Scouts of America come with a band, and they play music on those steps."

"Oh yes, I know about that," he responded, "but I've told them they can only play 'My country 'tis of thee,' and that's it."

He was in his dotage, and it was hopeless. Subsequently, the Quakers petitioned Congress, asking members to join them in exercising their right to protest the war on the House steps. Four members of Congress did so, and I was one of the four. I still have a picture of me sitting on the steps of the House of Representatives, supporting the daily reading of the names. I used that picture for my Christmas card that year. As each Quaker began to read, he or she was arrested and taken away by the Capitol police. Finally, when all the Quakers were arrested, the last one handed me *The Congressional Record*, and I started to read. I didn't miss a beat, and yet nothing happened. I was allowed to keep reading, uninterrupted. The chief of the Capitol police force was there. I turned to him and said, "Why don't you arrest me?"

"Why should I arrest you?" he said.

"Why did you arrest them?" I said, pointing to the Quakers.

"We arrested them because they were engaging in a breach of peace," he replied. "They were reading when they were directed not to."

I said, "Well, I'm reading from the same *Congressional Record.* I'm calling out the same names of the war dead. I'm doing the exact same thing. Why don't you arrest me?"

"When you do it," he said, "it's not a breach of the peace."

I thought, Isn't that interesting? The same behavior, carried out by two different people, is regarded in two different ways when it suits the convenience of the authorities.

Soon after, the Quakers brought a lawsuit against the Capitol police, with the help of the American Civil Liberties Union. I testified as a witness. A federal court issued an order that the Quakers had a right, as everyone does, to petition their representatives under the First Amendment, and they were allowed thereafter to use the steps, although once they were allowed to do so it was no longer something they wanted to do, and so they stopped coming.

I wondered how Rudolph Giuliani would fare against the resolve of those Quakers, or in more outspoken times. First he blocked off City Hall to peaceful protesters, then he removed the official portraits of his harshest critics. I called City Council Speaker Peter Vallone, to enlist his outrage in opposition to the mayor's action. I'm a supporter of Peter Vallone, but I felt he should be more forceful on this issue. "Peter," I said, "you can't let this go on. Half of City Hall belongs to you." I told him that he and every member of the city council should be out on those steps, every day, with a clarion call to rival Cato's in the Roman Senate: *Delenda est Carthago!* Carthage must be destroyed! "You have to let the people know he's violating their civil rights," I urged, referring to Giuliani.

Vallone agreed that something should be done about Giuliani's mean-spirited tactics and pledged to take it up with the mayor immediately. Shortly thereafter, the mayor's office announced that city council members could hold press conferences on the steps of City Hall. I thought, That's not petitioning your representatives. That's using your office as a backdrop for a public announcement. It was unconscionable that Giuliani meant to pass off allowing city council members the right to use the steps as curing his earlier ban on the public use of those steps. What a charade! What about the opponents of city council members? Could they gather peaceably on the steps? Or what about people who are not opponents but simply interested parties who want to come down to City Hall and get attention paid to an issue? Under Abe Beame, many New Yorkers will recall, nobody came down to City Hall to stand on the steps to make a statement. People were allowed to come, but nobody did, because nobody cared. There was no point. City Hall was irrelevant in those days, but under my administration City Hall became important again, and it remains so today. Those steps have to be recaptured for the public. They're a powerful symbol, and they belong to all of us, not only to Rudy.

Giuliani's latest proposal is that the public be allowed to apply for a police permit to use the steps, on ten days' notice. Again, a ridiculous solution to what had never been a problem prior to this administration. Most press conferences have to be scheduled immediately to be relevant; after ten days, the issue is usually long gone.

And it's not just the steps that have been thrown into question. Giuliani has decreed that you cannot enter City Hall without an invitation, although City Hall has always been open to tourists. The lockdown extends to the nonoffice areas as well. There are public rooms all over City Hall, many with historic items of public interest. There is a room called the Governors' Room, where I was told they planned to relocate my picture, along with David Dinkins's. (They wound up placing the portraits in a hallway area just outside the bathroom, along with the other "removed" mayors.) The Governors' Room contains George Washington's desk, but the room is always locked. It would have been like being in Siberia. That's Giuliani's Gulag for prior mayors, although for the time being we have been spared.

On a personal level, I don't much care where they put my portrait. It happens to be a very flattering picture of me, but I know what I look like, and the people of New York City know what I look like. And do you know what? Long after I'm gone, the people of New York City will still know what I look like. If they're interested, they can see various pictures of me, plus my old but beloved sports jacket, at the Museum of the City of New York. The La Guardia and Wagner Archives has my congressional and mayoral files as well as many photographs. The City Archives has hundreds of photographs taken during my twelve-year mayoralty. The point, really, is that Giuliani conducts himself as though the legacy of New York City politics is his to play with. If you cause him trouble, you're relegated to the Gulag, or to the area in front of the bathroom. It's a perfect example of the old aphorism that power corrupts and absolute power corrupts absolutely. Thankfully, we do not vest our mayors with absolute power, but Rudy is as corrupt in the use of power as they come.

There followed, predictably, a public squabble, and this was one time I didn't mind sinking to Giuliani's level. I knew I could never sink *all the way* to his level, so it wouldn't hurt my reputation to get down and dirty a little bit. Giuliani even thought to mimic me, in an unflattering way — as reported in one of Adam Nagourney's "Political Memo" columns in *The New York Times* — and so I parried by comparing him to Torquemada, the grand inquisitor of the Spanish Inquisition. Torquemada, Caligula, Pinochet . . . I wasn't sure which comparison was more appropriate, but they all seemed to fit, in their own way.

Some weeks later, Peter Vallone invited me to City Hall for his State of the City address, and I decided to take a little detour, thus beginning the second chapter of my "Blue Room" saga, and confirming that even your adversaries can sometimes surprise you. Once again, Giuliani and the people around him showed no shame in dealing viciously with whoever they felt was responsible for any negative publicity the administration received. People were streaming into City Hall, and I had a few minutes to spare, so I thought to take a look at the Blue Room. The renovation had been completed, I had been told it was very attractively done, and I wanted to see it for myself. After all, I'd spent so much time there as mayor it was only natural to want to see how the current occupant was keeping the place up. Instead of going upstairs, I went to the left, to the mayor's side of City Hall, where I was met by a young police officer. Actually, he couldn't have been *that* young, because he had been there when I was mayor. We recognized each other and smiled agreeably, and I said, "I'd like to see the Blue Room." I didn't think I needed to ask anyone's permission — because the Blue Room was a public room, and I was a member of the public — but this officer was clearly stationed as a keeper of the gate.

He said, "I'm sorry, Mayor, but I can't let you in. I'll have to get permission from the press secretary to have someone show you around."

I understood that, now that he'd brought

it up. It would have been the case for anybody, not just for me, but I couldn't see
asking for a private tour, just so I could have
a look around. So I said, "No, don't bother,
and don't feel bad about it. You're just
doing your job. I'll just go upstairs for
Speaker Vallone's address."

All I wanted was to go in, have a look, and
leave. I didn't want to burden anyone with
anything. It wasn't a big deal, and I might
have forgotten about it, but for the fact that
after the State of the City address I was
asked by a number of reporters for my comments. I offered some accolades to Vallone,
who I thought had delivered a fine speech,
and then Mary Gay Taylor of WCBS Radio
asked if I had been in to see the Blue Room
yet. I told the truth. "It's funny you should
ask," I said. "I tried." And then I told the
story.

Well, now they were all interested. I suppose I knew they would be, on some level,
but I wasn't thinking about it in
troublemaking terms. I wasn't thinking like
a journalist. A reporter asked me a simple
question, and I responded with the truth,
but underneath that truth was a headline:
The former mayor had been denied access
to one of the public rooms at City Hall. I
still didn't think it was a big story, but the

reporters saw things a little differently. The next morning, there was a nasty comment in the newspaper from Colleen Roche, Giuliani's press secretary. I was shocked. I had never met this young woman, as far as I knew, and yet she was quoted as saying, "If Koch had had a half-second's worth of patience, the guard would have gotten somebody of the appropriate stature to meet him at the gate."

Appropriate stature? What did I need with someone of appropriate stature? I just wanted to take a quick peek and leave.

The story didn't end there. Roche also said that I was a jealous man, that my jealousy was "palpable," that the condition of the Blue Room, and the city itself, was so much better than during my administration. She was over the top, in her vitriol. I thought, What have I ever done to this woman? Why is she lashing out at me in this way? I had never criticized her.

Of course that was all about to change. When a reporter called for my take on the brewing controversy I said, "It's shocking, the comments of this woman." Then I went and wrote a column about it, in which I called Roche's remarks "scurrilous." "The mayor and his minions have coarsened discourse in this city," I concluded. "It's time to remove the poster from that hot dog store window." I was referring to a poster on a window at Eighth Street and Sixth Avenue, praising Giuliani for his civility.

I have never believed that a civil servant or an appointed city employee has a right to criticize, with invective, another public official or public person. As press secretary, Colleen Roche could have reported that the mayor had said this, or the mayor had said that, but in my opinion she herself wasn't entitled to engage in a personal attack. She was not an elected official. She wasn't being paid by the taxpayers to criticize the mayor's critics. That was for the mayor to do, if he so chose. So I told reporters that though I didn't know this woman, I knew her by reputation, which was good, and by that reputation I reasoned that she could only have made such comments out of fear, or because she'd been told to do so by Cristyne Lategano, the mayor's communications director and Roche's superior, or by the mayor himself. "And we all know," I said, "that nothing is said on behalf of the mayor without the mayor's having cleared it. It's just outrageous."

Look, I'm not going to tell you I've never lied in my life, but I've probably lied the least of any public official that anyone could name. And I don't *like* to lie. And when Mary Gay Taylor asked me that question, it called for an answer. I didn't gild the lily, I didn't exaggerate. I was well aware that my little anecdote would cause a stir, but that wasn't my motivation. It was an amusing aside. What should have happened, if these people had any class whatsoever, was that someone from the mayor's office would have called my office and invited me down for a tour of the Blue Room. That would have been the commonsense thing to do, after the fuss had died down. The mayor himself might have called. Or Colleen Roche, or Cristyne Lategano. But instead the story was left to simmer, and then fade, and I imagine it was Giuliani's hope that I would fade along with it.

I mention these related stories because they take us back to the underlying theme of this book: remaining relevant. Do you think anybody would have bothered to report such nonsense if people hadn't come to see me as part of the ongoing life of the city? I was still on the map, still working effectively, still making a difference. What was telling, to me, was that the Blue Room story got more attention the next morning than Peter Vallone's State of the City speech and, while I felt bad to some extent about the distraction, it really provided a laugh or two. I didn't even mind that some people might have thought my actions petty, because those who know me know that I am not petty. Those who know me know that I have my father's temper. I am more forgiving than he ever was, but it takes a lot for me to forgive. I will not let a slight go unnoticed. My being denied access to the Blue Room was no slight at all — it was simply a silly City Hall policy, applicable to everyone, being carried out without interpretation by a civil servant. The slight came in the public scolding that followed, in the fact that the mayor felt it was necessary to attempt to undermine my reputation with his nasty attitude.

Let's be honest, I don't need Rudy Giuliani to uphold my legacy in New York City. Let him display my official portrait anywhere he wants — or nowhere at all, if that's what he chooses. I don't think I'm arrogant in believing that my place in history is assured, and I believe Giuliani knows this. And I am still adding to that history, to his consternation. It changes every day, because I change it every day, and there are new chapters still to come.

Ten

Epitaph

One of the more interesting side benefits to living a public life in a city like New York is knowing that your obituary is already written and filed away at the newspaper of record for when it's needed. It's a strange feeling to walk about knowing that someone at *The New York Times* has already written my obituary. It's like a kind of voodoo. I'm sure that some people in similar situations have gotten access to their obits, but there's something delicious about not knowing — and something a little bit morbid, or final, about finding out. Still, I do wonder about mine.

I have some idea how it will read. And I can guess how it will play. It'll probably start on the front page — and hopefully it'll be quite positive in tone. Even my critics will agree that I've done some good things for the city, and I hope that when I'm gone I am remembered in a positive light. I've thought about this from time to time, and obviously amended my thinking based on my various accomplishments. Back when I was a congressman, for example, I would never have presumed I'd get a lengthy obituary, but once you're elected mayor the famous words "Attention Must Be Paid!" suggest themselves.

Don't get me wrong, I have no expectation that my obituary will be anything like that given to, say, Frank Sinatra. I read Sinatra's obituary in the *Times* and thought, This is nuts. Three pages! Nobody will ever have an obituary like that. Presidents don't rate obituaries like that. It was just ridiculous. Granted, Sinatra was an extraordinary entertainer, and he deserved a first-rate obituary, but nobody deserves three pages. Sinatra, Elvis Presley, Jacqueline Onassis, Joe DiMaggio . . . I don't care who it is. Me, I'll settle for one full page, after the jump from page one, some flattering comments from friends and associates, a couple of nice photos from different points in my career, and no advertisements at the bottom of the page to poach on my posterity.

Recently, I was asked by the editors of

Vanity Fair magazine to supply my own obituary for their pages, in a jocular vein, and I used the occasion to reflect on the life I've lived and what I still hope to accomplish. I submitted the material and was told that the editors liked it. I told them I wanted to use the obituary as the ending to this book, and that I always ask publishers of my material to provide libel insurance because it is so easy to sue today, and every lawsuit costs money, even frivolous ones. They declined to publish the material because of the indemnity requirement, so the obit is appearing here for the first time. As you can see, my tongue was definitely in my cheek when I fulfilled their request, but I managed to stumble across some hidden insights despite myself.

Here's what I wrote:

When you read this obituary, I will have crossed over. I'm a believer in God, so I expect there will be one more career in my future. As I write this missive, a few minutes from death at the age of eighty-seven, I look back on my professional career knowing that nowhere else in the world would I have had the opportunities given to me in this extraordinary country, the United States of America.

My parents, whom I hope to see again in some form other than their earthly bodies, gave me my genes, formed my character, and between the two of them created my personality and intelligence. Whatever they did or had within them and passed on to me, I'm sure it is primarily responsible for my becoming a congressman from the Silk Stocking district in Manhattan and ultimately the 105th mayor of New York City.

I was always a shy child, and when I was thrust upon the public stage, I drew on my inner strength. In order to lead the city away from the brink of bankruptcy, I overcame my reticent nature and became, by intent, a major presence on the city stage, giving New Yorkers a sense that someone was in charge who would lead them across the desert toward a future that would benefit them and, even more, their children. During my twelve years as mayor — and only two other mayors before me, Fiorello La Guardia and Robert Wagner, had ever served for three terms — I was referred to as the quintessential New Yorker.

I considered the appellation at odds with my view of myself. In my private life, I avoided large parties and certainly was never part of the "beautiful people" scene. Nor did I ever crave wealth, even though after I left office, I became wealthy as a result of my third career, which included radio, television, columnists, and movie reviewer. I have written eleven books; the last one, I'm Not Done Yet!, *was a runaway bestseller encouraging people not to retire at age sixty-five but to continue working as long as their health held out.*

The New York Times *editorially referred to me as a "media conglomerate." The most satisfying comment I heard many times after leaving office, having been defeated in 1989 by David Dinkins when I ran for a fourth term, was "Mayor, you must run again," to which I replied with enormous pleasure every time, "No, the people threw me out and now the people must be punished."*

My last official act was done while presiding over The People's Court, *and using my legal authority as a former mayor to perform marriage ceremonies. I officiated at the marriage of Oprah Winfrey and her longtime friend Stedman Graham.*

I regret that I leave no heirs. Even more, I regret that I never entered into a permanent relationship so as to have the comfort of a partner at the close of my life. Nevertheless, my regrets are few.

In the eighty-seven years allotted to me, I

served with great pride for three years during World War II, drafted as a nineteen-year-old in the 104th Combat Infantry Division, receiving the Combat Infantry Badge and two battle stars. I ended my professional career as a partner in the law firm of Robinson Silverman Pearce Aronsohn & Berman, maintaining a small circle of friends including Judge Allen G. Schwartz, my law partner Jim Gill, and my doctor Bruce Barron. My sister Pat Thaler, and her husband, Al, are the executors of my estate.

For most of my adult life, I had only two requests of the Almighty: that when my allotted time had been expended, he would take me at once — no salami tactics — and it would be without prolonged pain. He granted me those requests. Had he not, I planned to spend my last few weeks in Oregon. I would like to have as my epitaph and on my headstone: "He was fiercely proud of his Jewish faith. He fiercely defended the City of New York and he fiercely loved the people of the City of New York."

Obviously, I meant the piece to be taken at least somewhat in jest, which explains the reference to Oprah Winfrey and her boyfriend, and the contention that the book you now hold in your hands will be a big hit.

282

(Who knows, maybe I'll be prescient in this latter regard.) The assumption, too, was that I would have all my faculties at the time of my death, which in my case is more than an assumption — it is my fervent wish. I thought I'd die at about eighty-seven, which was my father's age when he passed away, and I figured I'd still be presiding as judge on *The People's Court*. A fifteen-year run seemed to me about right. (Obviously, I was wrong in that regard.)

However, beyond my attempt at jocularity, I believe there are some important truths to be found in what I wrote. In the first place, I noticed that as I put those words down on paper I still thought of myself as a politician. But that is surely not surprising. With everything I've done since leaving office, I still regard my accomplishments in mayoral terms. By eighty-seven, God willing, I will have been out of office for more years than I served as an elected official, in any capacity, but it will be my work in government and politics that defines me. Being mayor will have been my most important time. And, undoubtedly, that's how others will think of me as well. Without question, being the three-term mayor of New York City will stand as the sum of my life, no matter what I go on to do next.

There are some people, like Byron White or Jack Kemp, both terrific athletes, who first make a name for themselves in one field and then become better known and make a greater contribution in some other field. That won't be the case with me, I'm fairly certain. With White and Kemp, just to continue those examples, their first marks were not their best marks — and only Dr. Freud would know why I selected two superb jocks to illustrate my point. In my case, my first mark was a bull's-eye.

Another aspect that stood out was that I realized I was starting to think of myself as an older person. Chronology aside, I've never considered myself elderly. I really haven't. For the longest time, I had a picture in my mind of how I saw myself, and I was always twenty-four. For some reason, that's the freeze-frame reflection I carried around in my head, and I held it there for the longest time. After the corruption crisis at City Hall, which I believe precipitated my stroke, I felt much older; and unlike Candide, I would never again feel as if I were living in the best of all possible worlds.

When you've lived a public life, people occasionally ask you what actor you'd like to see play your part in a movie based on your life. It's a fun question, and I've heard it a lot, but I mention it here because it nicely illustrates how the rest of the population gets older while we ourselves stay the same age in our mind's eye. I used to think Paul Newman would be an excellent choice — because the resemblance is uncanny. Then, when he started to get a little too old for the part, I moved to Robert Redford. Eventually, he got a little long in the tooth, too, so I figured Richard Gere would be right for the role. Of course, he's now also gotten along in years, so when I was asked recently who might play me, I had to recast the part again, and this time I chose Brad Pitt. It's an evolving thing. You go through life, you don't solve problems totally. You don't answer questions to put them to rest. Everything keeps repeating. Soon, I'm sure, even Brad Pitt will be too old for the role, and some well-meaning friend or reporter will pose the question again, and I'll have to look around for someone younger. How about Leonardo DiCaprio? Then again, if we were seriously discussing the selection of actors, I would revert to my first selection of years ago — Paul Newman.

The other, deeper truth between the lines of my obituary was pointed out to me by my sister Pat. I sent her a copy of the piece, just to have her thoughts, and she told me it struck her as sad. I thought, So much for my attempt at humor. But then she explained her feelings and I understood. My "regrets," which I glossed over for *Vanity Fair*, might indeed be few, but as Pat lovingly pointed out, they are mighty big ones. No, I did not take a partner, and at this time in my life it weighs on me. I am beginning to realize, finally, what I have missed — what I am missing, still. Projecting out over the next fifteen years, I imagine it will sadden me even more. In this respect, I was struck by a comment offered by Joe DiMaggio's brother, upon the Yankee legend's death. He said Joe's greatest regret was that he did not have a "constant companion." I feel the same way, but Joe DiMaggio was smarter than I — or certainly luckier. He had a "constant companion" for at least part of his long life.

Let me be brutally frank — or why else this book? It's a lonely thing, to grow old alone. It's a lonely thing, to take your dinners alone, more often than not. I'm lucky, in the sense that my days are so full that, on balance, it's easy not to notice that no one is waiting for me when I step in my apartment door. Besides, by the time I return home I'm usually too tired for much more than a quick bite and some public-television viewing. I'll spend three or four nights each week having dinner with friends, but often those friends are married couples. Let me tell you, there's a special kind of loneliness in being dropped at the front door of your apartment building, alone, while the rest of your party makes its way home in pairs.

What is it about our culture that makes dinner such a social meal? People think nothing of eating breakfast alone, or taking a quick lunch at their desks, but for some reason the evening meal is tied up with notions of family, and friendship, and romance. It's become a kind of barometer of how we're doing on an interpersonal basis. I don't dwell on it. I'll cook myself a steak or open a can of tuna, and be perfectly happy eating dinner in front of the television, lying down on my bed, bone tired. It's a fine, quiet transition from a long day that started at 5 A.M., and it doesn't usually happen more than three or four nights per week, so I'm not complaining. What I won't do, though, is go out to a restaurant by myself to have dinner. The idea is so foreign to me. I know there are millions of people who do it all the time, and I don't mean to question their routines, but I can't think of anything more depressing. If I'm going to sit by myself, I might as well be at home.

Let me move on to the next relevant point: I'm well aware of the occasional speculation regarding my sexual orientation, but it doesn't matter to me whether people think I'm straight or gay. Those who seek to "out" people who may or may not be gay can be described as comparable to the Jew catchers of Nazi Germany. The point I mean to make here is that I'm alone. In fact, I intentionally worded the mock obituary so that it could apply to heterosexuals and homosexuals alike, because having a companion certainly makes growing old and facing an uncertain future a whole lot easier. Life is gentler and more comforting when you have someone to share it with. In my case, it wasn't meant to be, although it is only lately that I find myself reflecting on it. I honestly didn't think about it much when I was younger, but I do now.

I know I've missed the pleasure of sharing triumphs and tragedies, of committing myself to someone else and having that commitment returned. Of course, there's the old Freudian reference to sublimation, which suggests that a life alone in some way allows your creative powers to expand. So my suggestion to any young person, male or female, straight or gay, is that it's always worth taking a chance on someone else and building a life together. No matter the failure rate, which is now about 60 percent, it's worth the shot, and if it turns out you made a mistake or a bad choice you can always correct it with another one.

I have, from time to time, thought of getting a dog. I had a dog once — a beautiful boxer I brought home with me from Germany after World War Two. But in those days you were not required to pick up after a dog on the streets of New York City, which as most people know is the law today. And a cat? I have a slight cat phobia. I'm uncomfortable when one is in the room, and cats can tell this about me, I'm convinced. They generally come over and sit nearby, or on my lap, to torture me.

There are, naturally, certain carryover concerns that result from being alone at this stage in my life, and the most pressing is how to manage if I am no longer able to care for myself. This is a tough one, and what I've chosen to do about it is quite practical. As I wrote earlier, I've taken out an insurance policy designed to pay for my nursing home or home health care needs. A lot of people my age are looking to these policies, and they're especially useful for people who don't have partners. Lifelong companions — husbands and wives, or same-sex partners — don't usually worry about their nursing home needs because they expect to die at home, in each other's care. There are always catastrophic illnesses to worry about, and certain chronic conditions that can drain a couple's resources, but the vast majority of married or partnered Americans end their lives at home. At least they do if they're the first to go. The surviving spouse will have to face some of the decisions I am facing now, but while they're both healthy and active it's often not an issue.

For me, though, it's an issue, and at first I wasn't sure I'd be able to find a suitable policy. With my medical history — a stroke, a pacemaker — I worried that I wouldn't find an insurance company willing to take me on, but I finally did and now I have the assurance of knowing that I won't have to spend down my assets in order to pay for care. There'll be enough coverage to pay most of the bills at the nursing home of my choice, and right now I have two in mind. There's a Jewish nursing home in Riverdale, right on the Hudson River. It's an excellent facility, in a pretty setting, and I'm confident it would take good care of me. However, there's also a Catholic home, Mary Manning Walsh, that right now is my first choice in Manhattan. It also gets excellent reviews, in every respect, but what I like about it is that it has an open bar for residents every afternoon. I don't drink, except socially, but it's such a nice touch. (Both nursing homes are nonsectarian.)

Alongside not taking a partner, of course, comes the regret over not having any children, which I mentioned in the *Vanity Fair* obituary, although not at great length. From a purely practical standpoint, now that I'm finally at a stage in my various careers where I'm making money, it would be nice to be able to leave it to my own children. You can't take it with you, and while I'm happy to leave my estate to my nieces and nephews and their children, it would be nice if I had children and grandchildren of my own to benefit from my successes.

As long as I'm on the subject, let me state that I enjoy children, and they seem to enjoy me. I think it's because I don't talk down to them, the way many adults are inclined to do. I didn't do so well with older people when I was a public official, and I think I know why: Without realizing it, I treated them like children, and they didn't like that. I don't blame them. I used to be overly solicitous of their feelings, to the point where my efforts came across as patronizing. Once, I called an elderly woman "Mama," and she shot me a withering glance and said, "I'm not your mother." I thought, Boy, is she smart! She put me right in my place.

I've worked on my failures in this area over the years, but with children, I've never had to work at it. I've always treated them with absolute respect for their intelligence. Now, whenever I think of my not having children, my first impulse is to regard the children I never had as little kids. Of course, my children would all be grown by now, they'd be parents or perhaps even grandparents themselves, so what I find I miss in this regard is the legacy aspect of parenthood, the feeling of immortality some people experience through their children. Interestingly, I've never had any desire to mentor a child. I suppose I have stood as a kind of role model to various younger people over the years, at least in the generic sense, but I've always rejected the notion of a formal mentoring relationship. It's not for me. I'm not interested in being a surrogate father to someone; I would not find it gratifying to take on a protégé.

Now, having said all of this and having acknowledged the hole that exists in my life because I never found a partner, I am well aware that a great many people my age somehow manage to meet other people and go on to enjoy their old age together. But I'm discounting that possibility in my case. Why? Because I don't believe it was meant to be, and I'm not seeking for it to happen.

Lest ye conclude by my closing remarks that I am depressed or unhappy, let me assure you that I am not. I simply wanted to tell the truth, the whole truth, and nothing but the truth. I have had a good life — not a perfect life, but an enjoyable and productive one — and it is not over. Many more challenges await me. Let me close with a cliché: I've done it, and will continue to do it, my way.

Coda

My Lazarus Heart

As many of you have no doubt read, I suffered my first heart attack in July 1999, while the book you now hold in your hands was being prepared for publication. After I was stable and resting comfortably, I thought about the book. Was the incident not only a part of my life but also worth reporting to you? Is there a lesson that has some universality attached? When my mind wandered to this book, I thought I should be taking notes, because what I was going through was directly related to the themes discussed in these pages. What follows, then, is a brief account.

If I were Catholic, I'd start in by telling you how I heard the voice of my guardian angel, cautioning me to "listen to your body" as I was exercising at the gym. But

I'm Jewish, and the voice I heard was that of my cardiologist, Dr. Joe Tenenbaum. Before that, at about six o'clock on Thursday morning, July 1, I felt a twinge in my chest as I left my apartment for the gym. That's not so unusual at age seventy-four, but I sensed that something was wrong. As soon as I began exercising on the treadmill, my awareness of danger quickened. My chest was tightening, yet like so many others similarly situated, I thought, It will go away. But Dr. Tenenbaum's voice was starting to come through even stronger. When I moved on to the weight machines, his voice in my head became louder. The tightening in my chest became more painful, and I asked my trainer to call EMS and get an ambulance.

My taking quick action, not delaying and hoping the pain would go away, undoubtedly saved me from a catastrophe. I listened to my body telling me to stop, and I sought help — if not immediately, close to it. In cases of coronary blockage, time means muscle loss. This was a phrase I heard throughout my nine-day treatment in the hospital. The earlier the intervention, the less damage is inflicted on the heart muscle, since the muscle dies if it is not regularly perfused — bathed in blood. Moreover, had I been taken to Columbia-

Presbyterian Hospital, where my cardiologist is located, as I originally requested of the EMS technician, it would have taken at least another half hour for the ambulance to get there, and I would have been caught in an electrical crisis visited on Washington Heights several days later, which cut all electricity to the hospital. New Yorkers will remember that July Fourth weekend as one of the hottest in the city's recent history, with temperatures running over 100 degrees. The blackout that subsequently covered Washington Heights and Columbia-Presbyterian Hospital undoubtedly would have limited some of the procedures that were needed and were performed at New York Hospital/Cornell, where I was taken instead. Indeed, about five days into the heat wave and electrical crisis, Columbia-Presbyterian began sending heart patients to its now sister hospital, New York/Cornell, where I was resting comfortably. I set this out as a reminder that our first impulses are not always the wisest. In this case — who knows? — a trip to my original hospital of choice might have had substantial adverse effects.

One thing is certain: it would have cost me travel time. We arrived at the New York Hospital/Cornell emergency room at 7:50

A.M., and I was in the cardiac catheter-ization laboratory within forty minutes. Six-teen minutes later, an angioplasty had been performed on one of my coronary arteries, which was 100 percent blocked. Doctors also determined that the flow of blood through the other two arteries had been re-duced (in one by 20 percent, in the other by 70 percent), and these conditions were to be treated with drugs and a change in diet.

One of the remarkable aspects of my treatment and outcome was described to me by my doctor at New York/Cornell. Two days after the angioplasty, Dr. Stephen Scheidt told me that my heart attack could be described as moderate. He noted that sometimes the heart muscle is stunned soon after a heart attack, appearing dead but ca-pable of reviving itself. Several days after the angioplasty, he ordered a nuclear stress test, which suggested that much of the front of my heart muscle had died. Dr. Scheidt esti-mated that the destruction of my heart muscle had reduced its pumping effective-ness by at least 20 percent. But a day later, a follow-up scan, automatically scheduled by hospital protocols, was taken, and Dr. Scheidt told me with some amazement that my heart "lit up like a Christmas tree" — showing life. As a result, he ordered an angioplasty for my second artery (the one that had 70 percent blockage) to let it pump even more blood to what I referred to as my "Lazarus heart." With the passage of time, Dr. Scheidt said, the original estimate of damage might be considerably scaled down.

A distressing aspect of my condition was that the monitoring machine attached to my body on day one revealed that I had sustained a short cycle of ventricular tachycardia. This type of abnormal heartbeat or arrhythmia, if it occurs for a long time, can cause death. Some irregularity of heartbeat following a heart attack is not infrequent, especially if the extra beats end within forty-eight hours of the initial attack; then their effects are, for the most part, inconsequential. However, when the arrhythmia continues after forty-eight hours, as it did with me, the patient has only a 15 percent chance (one chance in seven!) of surviving the heart attack. Many patients who survive initially will die within the next eighteen months of ventricular arrhythmia. But Dr. Bruce Lerman at the hospital explained to me that since much of my heart muscle was stunned rather than dead, the automatic protocol requiring the placement of a defibrillator in my body had to be reconsidered. The odds of an attack of ventricular arrhythmia after I left the hospital would be substantially reduced because of the revival of the heart muscle. When my heart muscle appeared to be dead, my doctors had said the odds were high that arrhythmia would occur after I left the hospital, particularly since they were able to produce such arrhythmia artificially by stimulating my heart. Now that the heart was alive, they thought they would try the stimulation procedure again and see if they got a different, nonarrhythmic result.

I said to Dr. Lerman, "What difference does it make?" I told him I would rather have the assurance of the defibrillator, regardless of the test results and the odds. I preferred the extra security.

Dr. Lerman agreed with my decision and placed a defibrillator in the right side of my chest. My old pacemaker was replaced, moved from the left to the right side of the chest, and incorporated in the new instrument. As the details of the procedure were explained to me, I couldn't help but marvel at modern medical technology. I thought, Those crazy congressmen in Washington don't give a damn about funding the New York hospitals that have made the United States number one in so many areas of medicine. They prefer to assist special interests that will reward them with campaign contributions.

On the Fourth of July, I watched the fireworks from my hospital room and recalled how, as mayor, I used to take a police launch from Gracie Mansion down the East River, where half a million New Yorkers always gathered to watch the show. I stood on the boat, pumped my arms up and down, and yelled, "It's me! It's me!" I will always remember the generous and joyous response from the crowd (it's called bonding), but the memory was especially sweet as I lay in my bed that night. I thought, It's me! It's still me! And it'll take more than a modest heart attack to keep me from the grand spectacle that is New York City — and my ever-changing role on its front lines.

God has kept his word to me. He has not taken me one slice at a time. I intend to keep my bond with Him and use my allotted time in a positive way. The untimely and tragic death of John F. Kennedy, Jr., at age thirty-eight brought home to me with even more emphasis how fragile we all are, and posed for me every day a question that will probably never be answered: Why was I saved? The simple response is that God is not yet finished with me, and I remain relevant.

The employees of Thorndike Press hope you have enjoyed this Large Print book. All our Large Print titles are designed for easy reading, and all our books are made to last. Other Thorndike Press Large Print books are available at your library, through selected bookstores, or directly from us.

For information about titles, please call:

(800) 223-1244
(800) 223-6121

To share your comments, please write:

Publisher
Thorndike Press
P.O. Box 159
Thorndike, Maine 04986

I9780786228911
LT B KOCH
Koch, Ed,
I'm not done yet! :

HQ
MID-YORK LIBRARY SYSTEM
1600 Lincoln Avenue
Utica, New York 13502
(315) 735-8328

A cooperative library system serving
Oneida, Madison, and Herkimer Counties
through libraries and a bookmobile.

010100

A00001O6522964